TRAVELCARD WALKS IN WEST LONDON

TRAVELCARD WALKS
IN WEST LONDON

Margaret Sharp

MAINSTREAM
PUBLISHING

EDINBURGH AND LONDON

Copyright © Margaret Sharp, 2000
All rights reserved
The moral right of the author has been asserted

First published in Great Britain in 2000 by
MAINSTREAM PUBLISHING COMPANY (EDINBURGH) LTD
7 Albany Street
Edinburgh EH1 3UG

ISBN 1 84018 312 8

Maps by Jeremy Sharp
Photographs by David Sharp

A catalogue record for this book is available from the British Library

Typeset in Futurist and Garamond
Printed and bound in Great Britain by Creative Print Design Wales

To my friends the Tuesday Walkers
of Chiswick Adult Education Class
Walks in West London

Contents

Introduction

These walks explore the many and varied open spaces within the western half of Greater London – its parks, commons, fields, hillsides and woodlands, linked by footpaths, waterways and green corridors. As well as these natural features, the walks visit also some of the old village centres of Middlesex and Surrey which have survived, surrounded by suburbia but not altogether obliterated. Places such as Petersham and Barnes south of the Thames, and Ruislip and Pinner to the north are all worth visiting in their own right as well as being the gateways to some beautiful walks.

All the starting points for these walks can be reached from anywhere in London by Tube, rail or bus, and all the walks begin and end within London Travelcard zones, even if they visit places outside. So, once you have your Travelcard for the appropriate zones, you can get back home without paying a penny more on fares, wherever you end up. And London OAPs holding the Freedom Pass will have no fares to pay at all.

The majority of the basic routes are between 3 and 5

miles long, fitting comfortably into a morning or afternoon, or providing a refreshing evening stroll in summer after work. Routes can also be combined to give a longer walk, and sometimes extensions are suggested that will take you further afield. Some of these extensions on the outer fringes of London would take you right out into the country via the Ruislip woods or Epsom Common. But even a 3- or 4-mile walk can provide a genuine country experience – as in the wild Ham Riverside Lands, or from the top of Barn Hill across the medieval hedge boundaries of Fryent Fields.

Each walk is accompanied by a sketch map of the route. The OS Landranger map 176 (West London 1:50,000) covers all the walks in this book and will help with placing each route in relation to its locality, and in identifying landmarks. If you intend to leave the route sketched, it would be advisable to take the All-London Bus Map (or a local version) and either a street atlas or the appropriate sheet of a series of folding street maps of Greater London. These are about 3 inches to the mile and, by showing street names, enable you to find your way easily to bus stop, station, pub, Great Aunt Mary's house or whatever. Other than this no special equipment is needed.

Wear any shoes that you find comfortable and sturdy enough. In wet weather make sure the soles have sufficient grip – smooth soles may leave you slipping helplessly in mud or on a grassy slope.

You don't have to stick strictly to the routes suggested

here. So many areas are worth returning to again and again to explore further and find alternative paths and to enjoy the many lovely views and areas of countryside still remaining in West London.

Travelling in London

The best way to travel across London to start these walks is by public transport. The London Underground (the Tube), buses and national railway link all parts of London. London north of the Thames is rather better served by the Tube than is the section to the south, but here there is a thick network of railway lines connecting the suburbs to central London via Victoria, Waterloo, Charing Cross and other terminuses, and interchange stations which give direct access to the Tube.

TRAVELCARDS

These give passengers the freedom to make unlimited journeys on any and all of these systems plus the Docklands Light Railway (DLR). Travelcards can be transferred from bus to train to Tube and will take you through the automatic gates at some stations. Different types of Travelcard are available.

ONE DAY TRAVELCARD

Valid after 9.30 a.m. Mondays to Fridays and any time at weekends and on public holidays. There is a flat rate fare for children aged 5–15 and a varying fare for adults according to the number of zones travelled.

WEEKEND TRAVELCARD

Saves 25 per cent on the cost of two One Day Travelcards. Can be used for the two days of any weekend or on two consecutive days of a public holiday weekend.

FAMILY TRAVELCARD

Offers a saving on individual Travelcards for one or two adults travelling with up to four children, with a very low flat rate fare for the children. They need not be related but must travel as a group.

PERIOD TRAVELCARD

Available for a week, month or other period.

PHOTOCARD

Needed for all children aged 14 or 15 to obtain any child rate card. Adults need one for a Period Travelcard or seven-day bus pass only.

ZONES

The cost of all types of Travelcard depends on the number of zones travelled. You need to state when buying your card which zones it needs to cover. There are six zones, with Zone 1, Central London, being relatively more expensive. The details at the beginning of each walk in this book include the zones of the start and (where different) finish points, but walkers will need to add in the zones covered by their journey from home. The zone map in this book will enable you to work this out.

WHERE TO BUY YOUR TRAVELCARD

These can be bought at Tube stations, most London rail stations, LT Information Centres and at selected pass agents, which are usually local newsagents displaying the pass agent sign.

BUSES

In January 2000, new, simplified bus fares were introduced. Currently, the fare for a single journey including the Central Zone is £1.00; any journey outside costs 70p. One-day and seven-day bus passes covering any number of journeys are available.

INFORMATION

You should be able to obtain at any Underground booking office a copy of the Tube map and the folder 'Travelling in London'. This folder contains details of fares, cards and passes and a fold-out map of zones showing all stations.

If you begin with Walk 1 in this book you can take advantage of the fact that it starts from Hammersmith station by visiting the LT Travel Information Centre upstairs in the bus station. Here you can obtain not only the Tube map and folder but also the All-London Bus Map and many of the local bus maps which have more detail and a larger scale. You can also obtain some of the local transport guides currently published by London Transport in conjunction with *Time Out* which give full details of all the transport, including a route plan of every bus route, and general information on shops, restaurants, theatres and other local amenities.

Bus maps and local transport guides are also available

in many public libraries and local Tourist Information Centres.

....

For further information on London Transport services ring 020 7222 1234.

For train times ring Rail Enquiries on 08457 48 49 50.

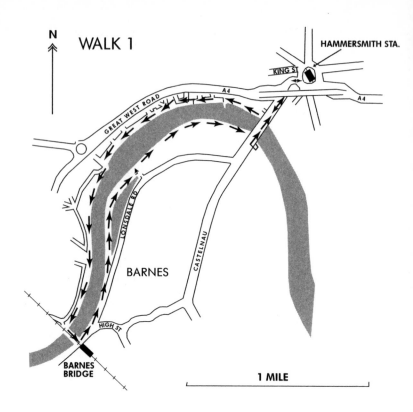

N

WALK 1

HAMMERSMITH STA.

KING ST

A4

GREAT WEST ROAD

A4

LONSDALE RD

CASTELNAU

BARNES

HIGH ST

BARNES
BRIDGE

1 MILE

Hammersmith and Chiswick Malls and Barnes Riverside

Hammersmith Broadway, the starting point of this walk, is a busy junction of cars, buses and Tube trains, yet within five minutes you can leave all this behind for a quiet riverside walk. The varied and elegant townscape of Hammersmith and Chiswick Malls contrasts with the view of the tree-lined towpath across the river. Returning on the Barnes side, the balconied houses of the Terrace give way to a rural stretch of towpath and the oasis of the Leg O'Mutton Reservoir – a wide, peaceful stretch of water fringed with bushes and reeds which has come to resemble a natural lake.

....

DISTANCE: 4.5 miles (circular). Connections with Walk 2 at Barnes Bridge station and Walk 3 at Chiswick Church.

TERRAIN: Pavements, then rough towpath.

REFRESHMENTS: Pubs and cafes at Hammersmith Broadway, Hammersmith Mall and in Barnes.

TRANSPORT: Piccadilly, District and Hammersmith and

City Lines. Buses 9, 10, 27, 33, 72, 190, 209, 211, 220, 266, 267, 283, 295, 391, H91, R69.

TRAVELCARD ZONE: 2

STARTING POINT: Hammersmith Piccadilly and District Line station.

From the street level of the station (the Broadway Centre), follow first the signs for Fulham Palace Road, keeping to the right of Tesco's store, but continue straight ahead to exit into tiny Bradmore Square, dominated by a restaurant in the shell of the original Bradmore House of 1739 – rather more dignified than its previous use as a bus garage! Bear right and cross the pedestrian crossing, then left over the next one to the left-hand pavement of Hammersmith Bridge Road or into the little public garden alongside with St Paul's Church on your left. Walk up, under the flyover, to Hammersmith Bridge. Do not cross the bridge but walk down the slope and turn right underneath it and along Lower Mall. Beyond Furnival Gardens pass The Doves into Upper Mall, noting this interesting old pub and also Kelmscott House which William Morris named after his Elizabethan manor house on the Upper Thames. Continue beside the river through an arcade to pass the Old Ship Inn and briefly inland down Hammersmith Terrace. At the far end you enter Chiswick Mall and pass a succession of grand 18th-century houses, notably Morton, Strawberry and

Walpole Houses, though the last-named, behind its 18th-century façade, is Tudor in origin. These face Chiswick Eyot where osiers (flexible branches from the willowtree) were grown for basket-making. Other 18th- and 19th-century houses in a variety of styles continue up to the end of the Mall.

At the junction with Church Street our path continues as a riverside walk through a small gateway beside the drawdock with a causeway from which the ferry to Barnes used to run. But take a few minutes first to look at St Nicholas Church and Hogarth's grave, prominent in the churchyard ahead. *Walk 3 leaves by Powell's Walk the other side of the church.*

A few yards up Church Street is a 16th-century house called the Old Burlington, formerly an inn and still with its cupboard to the right of the door for locking up drunks. The Lamb Brewery lies behind on the right and there is the delightful group of 17th-century cottages in Pages Yard just before the junction with the Great West Road. Round the corner, beyond the pub, is little Chiswick Square, a group of houses dating from about 1680 to each side of Boston House. Hogarth House, the painter's 'quiet country retreat', lies beyond the busy Hogarth Roundabout.

We return with relief to the peace of the riverside path. Through the gateway beside the drawdock a paved promenade goes in front of a large new estate. Beyond this the riverside path continues as a tarmac cycle track with an earthen footpath alongside. The cycle track joins a road, but keep on the path beside the river, past a long-disused bandstand and shelters. Cross the concrete slope in front of school boathouses (or go round behind them) and up steps to Barnes Bridge. Cross the bridge. On the far side, from the foot of the steps, turn right and cross with care to the flood-wall walkway – or use the pedestrian crossing at the foot of Barnes High Street. You are passing Barnes Terrace, a fine and varied line of houses mostly dating from the 1740s to the early 19th century, many with elegant wrought-iron balconies. Note the blue plaque to Gustav Holst who lived here from 1908 to 1913. *For Barnes Village, Pond and Green, see Walk 2.* Continue along the concrete walkway and when it ends at the towpath keep along the right-hand path facing you through a small public garden. Beyond the garden is the Leg O'Mutton Reservoir, now a local nature reserve. Turn in at the first entrance to the reservoir and bear left to walk the whole length of this lovely stretch of water, which is home to many waterfowl. Leave it by a gate at the far end, turn back to the river towpath and continue along the towpath back to Hammersmith Bridge (0.7 mile). The towpath continues to Putney, but to finish the walk go under the bridge, turn up to the pavement and cross the bridge to return by the outward route.

Barnes Village, Green and Common via Beverley Brook

Barnes kept its village centre intact when suburbia surrounded it. Its small-scale High Street still winds up from the river to the pond with its island and ducks, the old schoolhouse, and a strategically placed pub overlooking it. Around the pond lies the Green, one arm stretching towards Beverley Brook and the Common beyond – a rougher, wilder area where paths wind through gorse and brambles or over rough grass to woodland – the other arm stretching to the church. Several modest houses of the 17th, 18th and 19th centuries remain, lining the Terrace, overlooking the pond and continuing up Church Road. In the area of 19th-century artisans' cottages adjoining Mortlake, paved alleyways which cross over Beverley Brook and under the railway provide quiet, traffic-free routes through the built-up area, particularly delightful when the tiny front gardens are full of flowers.

....

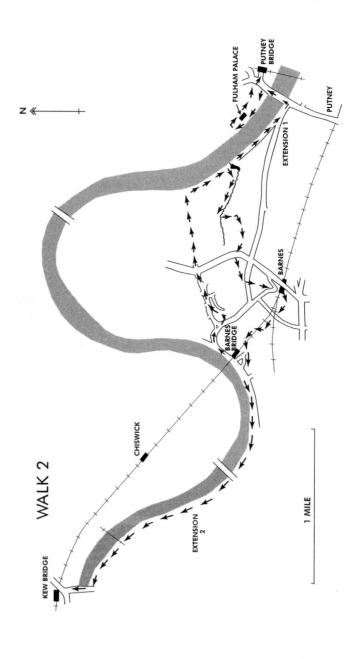

WALK 2

KEW BRIDGE

CHISWICK

EXTENSION 2

BARNES BRIDGE

BARNES

FULHAM PALACE

PUTNEY BRIDGE

PUTNEY

EXTENSION 1

N

1 MILE

DISTANCE: 3.5 miles (circular). Connection with Walk 1 at end.

EXTENSION 1: Bishops Park and Fulham Palace (2.5 miles).

EXTENSION 2: To Mortlake and Kew Bridge (2.2 miles).

TERRAIN: Some pavements, mostly earth and grass paths.

REFRESHMENTS: Pubs in Barnes. Light refreshments at tennis courts pavilion beside the Old Cemetery car park. Also in gardens on Putney Embankment and Bishops Park on Extension 1, and riverside pubs on Extension 2.

TRANSPORT: South West Trains. Buses 209, R69 (Mon–Sat) to Barnes Bridge; 33, 72, 265 to Barnes station.

TRAVELCARD ZONE: 3

STARTING POINT: Barnes Bridge station.

ALTERNATIVE STARTING POINT: Barnes station (begin at third paragraph below).

....

Turn right from Barnes Bridge station along Barnes Terrace, noting the blue plaque which records Gustav Holst's residence in one of these fine balconied houses, then curve round up the High Street to the pond. Opposite the Sun Inn, cross over and go round the right-hand side of the pond towards the old schoolhouse. Passing to the right of this, follow the path up the narrowing triangle of the Green to shops, then continue up Church Road, or the Crescent opposite with its exuberantly decorated 'lion houses'. Pass the church which has fine 18th-century houses each side: Strawberry House, originally the rectory, The Homestead and Homestead Cottage. The oldest part of the church dates back to about 1100, with a fine modern extension built after a fire. At the junction with Castelnau, cross straight over to Queen Elizabeth Walk to the right of the Red Lion pub, and continue down it between playing fields and the Wetlands Centre to the river. Turn right along the towpath. It ends at the footbridge over Beverley Brook on to Putney Embankment. *For extension to Bishops Park and Fulham Palace, see Extension 1.*

Do not cross the footbridge but turn up the path along the banks of Beverley Brook for 0.5 mile. The locked-off bridge now leading to a housing estate used to carry the drive to Barn Elms manor house, long demolished. Cross the brook by the second open footbridge beyond this and walk forward on to the Common. When the fence of Long Meadow on the right turns away, continue ahead on a path through scrub and trees, crossing over two paths, to a broad path coming from the open area of Putney Common. Turn right on this, past the wall of Putney Old Cemetery, and fork right alongside Barnes Old Cemetery, or on one of its paths through the tangle of shrubs and broken graves. All these paths eventually join a tarmac track beyond a small car park where you should turn right past WCs to Rocks Lane. Cross over to a tarmac path nearly opposite leading across Barnes Common. Ignore a succession of crossing paths until your path joins another major tarmac path, where you should turn left until you see a block of houses across a road. Cross with care to the driveway to the right of the white weather-boarded house which used to be the miller's house. (This block of houses is still called Mill Hill, though the 'hill' is a mere 27 feet above sea level and the windmill was blown down long ago.) Continue ahead on a narrow path over the Common, ignoring crossing paths, to Barnes station and go up steps beside the old station building to cross the footbridge.

If joining here, turn right on the footbridge from the steps up from the platform. On the far side, turn right and take the earthen path through a birch wood until you see through the trees on the right an open grassy area, a former cricket pitch. Cross this diagonally to a road and a level crossing on the far right. Go through the first crossing gate only, and turn into a small recreation ground and bowling green (WCs here). Go round it rightwards to an exit over Beverley Brook, turn right under a railway arch and left at a meeting path past a row of 19th-century cottages with pocket-handkerchief gardens. These paved pathways with their terraced cottages are a delightful feature of old Barnes and Mortlake. Continue on this path under two more railway arches out to a road, then down Thorne Passage, the second path on the right. The gardens in front of these cottages gradually increase in length because the path you are on follows the diagonal line of an ancient footway through the Barnes West Field, one of the old common fields, while the houses are set in the grid pattern of the streets, created when the land was built over in the latter half of the 19th century. Coming out at a road, take the path alongside the Church of St Michael and All Angels, and bear right then left down Elm Bank Gardens back to the river at Barnes Bridge. *Extension 2 continues from here. Connect here with Walk 1.*

EXTENSION 1: BISHOPS PARK AND FULHAM PALACE (2.5 MILES)

Cross the footbridge on to Putney Embankment and walk up it. Cross Putney Bridge and go down steps on the left into Bishops Park. Follow the riverside path known as Bishops Walk with its magnificent avenue of plane trees for 0.3 mile, then cross the grass to an iron gateway near a small aviary and refreshment pavilion. Go through the gateway and turn right through a stone gateway and down the drive. Go through the arch ahead for a view of the cobbled quadrangle of Fulham Palace. The Bishops of London had a residence here from Saxon times, but the quadrangle with its black and red brick diaper design is the oldest part of the present building, dating from the reign of Henry VII. Return through the arch, turn right and right again to go round the Palace buildings, past the small Museum, into the gardens. Beyond the lawn are the rose and herb gardens and a walled garden, sheltered and peaceful behind its ancient walls. Return through the stone and iron gateways back into Bishops Park and turn left to follow the line of the moat to pass almshouses and Fulham Parish Church back to Putney Bridge, and return down the Embankment to finish the main walk.

EXTENSION 2: ALONG THE TOWPATH TO MORTLAKE
AND KEW BRIDGE (2.2 MILES)

Cross the road in front of Barnes Bridge station, climb the steps over the flood wall and take the wooden walkway under the bridge on to the towpath. Continue on this, passing the White Hart's river frontage and the 19th-century buildings of Watney's brewery until you reach Chiswick Bridge. Some sections of this stretch of towpath are narrow and low-lying and thus apt to flood at very high tides, but there are plenty of steps and alleyways to take you into Mortlake High Street to bypass any floods. Beyond the Ship Inn and Chiswick Bridge the towpath widens and becomes more rural again, finishing with lovely views of Strand-on-the-Green across the river shortly before Kew Bridge. *Walk 4 continues beyond Kew Bridge.* You can return from Kew Bridge station (on the other side of the river) to Barnes Bridge or Barnes stations.

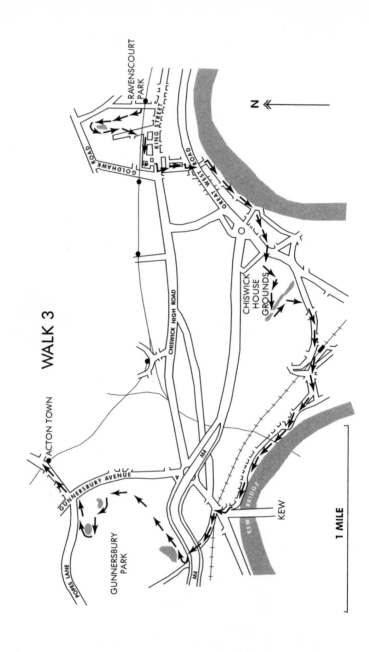

WALK 3

Ravenscourt Park, Chiswick House Grounds and Strand-on-the-Green

A very civilised walk, largely on pavements and tarmac, but including the green vistas of three delightful small parks, once country estates now oases of nature; linked by a couple of elegant squares and two particularly fine stretches of urban riverside.

....

DISTANCE: 4.0 or 5.5 miles (linear). Connection with Walk 1 at Chiswick Mall and Walk 4 at Kew Bridge.
EXTENSION: To Gunnersbury Park (1.5 miles).
TERRAIN: Hard surfaces throughout.
REFRESHMENTS: Numerous pubs. Cafes in Ravenscourt Park, Chiswick House Grounds and Gunnersbury Park.
TRANSPORT: District Line. Buses 27, 190, 267, 391, H91 to park gates.
TRAVELCARD ZONES: 2 and 3.
STARTING POINT: Ravenscourt Park station.

....

From the station exit turn right under the railway, cross the road, go through a gate into Ravenscourt Park then take a path on the right. *From King Street buses* enter by the main gates, follow a path under a railway arch and straight ahead.

Opposite the little tea house (WCs alongside) turn left and follow the path rightwards round the lake. Near the end of the circuit, leave the path just before a flowerbed and cross the grass to a diagonal path. Follow this rightwards to a gate out of the park. Turn left, under the railway, and right along Hamlet Gardens into Westcroft Square. Go round two sides of this fine square on to King Street, cross at traffic lights, then turn back a few yards to go into St Peter's Square, an elegant square from the 1830s. Cross to the garden in the centre, enter by the gate and walk the full length, passing the memorial sculpture, *The Greek Runner*. From the gate at the far end, turn left towards St Peter's Church, a Grecian-style building built in 1829. Just before the church, take a path to a subway under the Great West Road and turn down to the riverside. The arches ahead were part of the West Middlesex Waterworks and the main building is visible beyond. Turn right up Hammersmith Terrace and Chiswick Mall (as in Walk 1), but at St Nicholas Church climb the steps into the churchyard, pass Hogarth's tomb and follow the path round the church to take the walled Powell's Walk on the left. Turn left on the main road, cross and enter Chiswick House Grounds by the first gate.

There is plenty to see in these beautifully landscaped gardens, and the house is an exquisite Palladian villa built between 1727 and 1729. For a short route taking in at least some of the views, bear right, left and right again through a wooded area into the Italian Gardens, fronted by the conservatory famous for its camellias. Follow the curved hedge two-thirds of the way round, then walk ahead to the Inigo Jones gateway. The refreshment pavilion (Burlington's Cafe) and WCs lie to the left beyond it. Ahead lies the garden front of Chiswick House, the entrance on the far side. Even if you do not intend to visit the interior, the grand classical front with its great staircases should be viewed. The lawns beyond are covered in drifts of crocuses in the spring and there is a cascade at the head of the lake. Returning to the garden front, walk down the avenue between urns and sphinxes and under ancient cedars, then take the left-hand one of five paths radiating from its end, passing the Temple in its small amphitheatre. Cross the lake by the classical bridge and turn left along its bank until just past the Temple, then turn up a path leading to the Obelisk.

Leave the park by the gate beyond, turn right and continue along Burlington Lane to Chiswick station, cross the line by the footbridge, turn sharp right from the foot of the steps, curve round in front of a parade of shops and continue straight ahead down Grove Park Road, forking right at a church. You soon reach the open riverside at Strand-on-the-Green. Continue along the riverside pavement in front of old pubs and cottages and a few grander houses. Note Zoffany House (c. 1700), Zoffany's home from 1790 until his death in 1810. The pavement leads to Kew Bridge.

To return from here (4.0 miles), cross at the traffic lights rightwards for Kew Bridge station (South West Trains) or for buses back along Chiswick High Road to the start of the walk or to Hammersmith. *To connect with Walk 4*, cross Kew Bridge.

EXTENSION: TO GUNNERSBURY PARK (1.5 MILES)

Pass Kew Bridge station and turn left up Lionel Road just beyond. Cross Great West Road by subway, turn right from the exit, pass the battlemented gatehouse and go round the corner to enter Gunnersbury Park. Go ahead on the path to the right of the Potomac Lake, passing the Folly boathouse with its octagonal tower. Continue ahead on the path near the wall as far as a roofed shelter, then cross the grass to a fence and follow this rightwards to a crossing path. Turn right for a glimpse of the derelict stables and coach-houses, then left and left again past the rock garden to the Orangery. Beyond this, follow the path or cross the grass towards the Large Mansion. This is not the original Gunnersbury House, but was built in 1802 and much enlarged and embellished by Sidney Smirke in 1835 for Nathan Rothschild, remaining in the Rothschild family until the death of Leopold in 1937. It is now a local museum. Go left from the building (passing near WCs) to the Round Pond. Go round this to pass the Temple, built in the 1760s when Princess Amelia lived here and would use the Temple to entertain guests for tea. Follow a path down steps past the refreshment pavilion and out to the lawn in front of the Museum entrance. The Museum has many specialist collections reflecting local history and industries, and you can see the Rothschild carriages. Past the entrance, follow the path past the Small Mansion to the pedestrian gate out on to Gunnersbury Avenue, cross this at the traffic lights and continue ahead down Gunnersbury Lane to Acton Town station (District and Piccadilly Lines) and E3 buses.

CHISWICK HOUSE (English Heritage):
Open April–Sep (daily) 10a.m.–6p.m.
(closed 1p.m.–2p.m.);
Oct–March (Wed–Sun) 10a.m.–4p.m.
(closed 1p.m.–2p.m.).
Admission charges apply.

GUNNERSBURY PARK MUSEUM:
Open April–Oct (Mon–Fri) 1p.m.–5p.m.;
weekends and bank holidays 1p.m.–6p.m.;
Nov–March (daily) 1p.m.–4p.m.
Entrance: free.

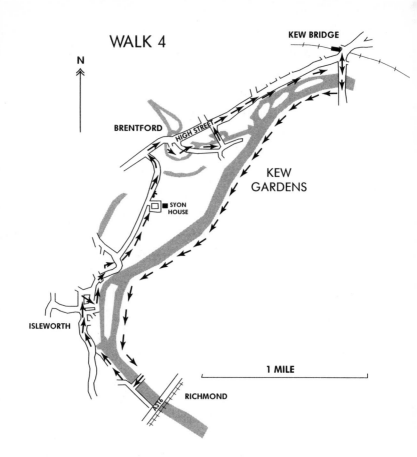

WALK 4

N

KEW BRIDGE

BRENTFORD

HIGH STREET

SYON
HOUSE

KEW
GARDENS

ISLEWORTH

1 MILE

A316

RICHMOND

Kew Circular via towpath, Isleworth and Syon Park

A walk that falls into two contrasting sections: the first is essentially a rural riverside walk alongside Kew Gardens and Old Deer Park, while the second section returns through a varied man-made environment – old village and new development in Old Isleworth, the grand house and park of the Duke of Northumberland and signs of Brentford's industrial past.

....

DISTANCE: 4.0 or 5.5 miles (circular). Connections with Walks 3 and 9.

EXTENSION: To Gunnersbury Park (as Walk 3).

TERRAIN: Towpaths and pavements.

REFRESHMENTS: Pubs at Kew Bridge, Isleworth and Brentford; cafeterias in Syon Park and Watermans Arts Centre, Brentford.

TRANSPORT: South West Trains to Kew Bridge station; District Line and Silverlink to Kew Gardens station (0.75 mile from starting point). Buses 65, 391 to Kew

Green, 237, 267 to Kew Bridge station. NB At weekends between June and September it may be possible to cross from the Kew towpath to Isleworth Church by ferry, shortening the walk by 1.5 miles.

TRAVELCARD ZONE: 3

STARTING POINT: Kew Bridge, Kew side.

....

From Kew Bridge station, cross the bridge. From Kew Green on the far side, drop down either side of the bridge to the towpath and turn left. Follow the towpath south-west towards Richmond for about 2.5 miles, passing Kew Palace and Gardens with views across to the Grand Union canal outfall and Syon Park. *Those hoping to use the ferry should look out for it opposite Isleworth Church* – there will be a notice if it is running. Otherwise, continue to Richmond Lock and cross the pedestrian bridge.

On the far side, go forward from the foot of the steps. When the road swings away from the river, continue on the paved Riverside Walk. The narrow paved path soon opens out into a pleasant strip of grass with trees and benches. Approaching Isleworth Ait the path leaves the riverside and turns up to Richmond Road. Turn right, crossing the River Crane, and follow the high wall of Nazareth House past the gates, which allow you a glimpse of house and grounds, to Old Isleworth.

Cross over to the Victorian drinking fountain, which has an attractive group of buildings behind. Just past the

Swan Inn, a diagonal path across Isleworth Green leads through an archway into Lower Square, dominated by the restored Old Blue School. Go down the left-hand side of the school, turn left to the river and round the river frontage of the Town Wharf pub. Beyond the pub, a pleasant new pathway (part of the Thames Path) with fine views down river brings you out through high, private-looking gates into Church Street, emerging where the Duke of Northumberland's River rushes over weirs into the Mill Pond before emptying into the Thames. This man-made river was cut from the River Crane in the 15th century to power the cornmill of Syon Abbey and acquired its present name when the Dukes of Northumberland took over the Abbey estates. A two-minute walk up Mill Plat leads to the Ingram Almshouses. Built in 1664, they are the oldest and most picturesque of Isleworth's many almshouses – a most worthwhile diversion.

Turn down Church Street to regain the Thames at the London Apprentice, a pub with a long history and a superb position. *The ferry lands here.* Turn into the churchyard, pass the church, mostly rebuilt after a fire in 1943, and look at the memorial to plague victims, under the ancient yew tree. Leave the churchyard down steps, turn left and cross the road to enter through the gates into Syon Park, which has a public footpath through it.

Walk on the path to the right of the road with views into the Rose Garden and to Syon House beyond the ha-ha, its four-square solidity giving no hint of the delicacy of its Robert Adam interiors. The park has many other attractions (most with entrance charges) such as the gardens, Grand Conservatory and Butterfly House, and is worth a separate visit. To leave the park, pass the Patio cafeteria and WCs and exit via the walled track to the main road. *To finish the walk here (4.0 miles)*, cross the road for buses 237 or 267 back to Kew Bridge.

To continue the walk, turn right towards Brentford and cross the bridge over the canal *where Walk 9 starts from the opposite side of the road.* A footpath sign points down to the canal towpath to the right. Follow this path alongside houseboats until it ends at a stairway over the wall. Continue along this higher path in front of new housing and an old warehouse, beyond which it curves round to The Ham. Go under the old railway bridge and up the slope and steps facing. Cross the canal by the footbridge, go down steps on the far side and follow the narrow path beside the canal to Thames Locks. (In icy weather keep on the path above it in front of flats). Thames Locks are the last locks on the Grand Union Canal before it joins the Thames.

Turn left over the canal and basin up Dock Road, noting the fan-shaped cobbles in the last stretch before Brentford High Street, where you should turn right. As you pass opposite the County Court, look for the monument, moved here from Ferry Lane, commemorating four major events when Brentford figured in national history. Keep on the main road to the pub on the corner of Ealing Road. Opposite this, turn down broad steps, left through high blue gates, round in front of offices, then up steps to the broad, high promenade on the river side of the Watermans Arts Centre. (Steps at the far end lead to cafeteria and WCs.) Continue through the riverside gardens with the tall tower of the Kew Pumping station ahead. The little 18th-century Charity School alongside the redundant church, now a Musical Museum, may be glimpsed up on the road, half-way along. At the end of the gardens, continue along the road for a few yards then turn down past a pub to some rough steps which take you back to the river at The Hollows, a riverside path lined with moored houseboats. Continue along the path back to Kew Bridge. *Walk 3 finishes here. Walk 9 connects at the canal bridge in Brentford.*

EXTENSION: TO GUNNERSBURY PARK

See the end of Walk 3 for Extension to Gunnersbury Park.

SYON HOUSE:
Open April–Oct (Wed, Thurs and Sun)
11a.m.–5p.m.,
Fri and Sat 11a.m.–3.30p.m.
Gardens open 10a.m.–6p.m. or dusk
(daily except 25 and 26 December).

WALK 5

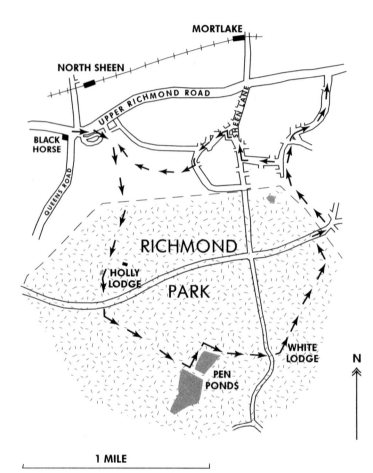

MORTLAKE

NORTH SHEEN

UPPER RICHMOND ROAD

SHEEN LANE

BLACK
HORSE

QUEENS ROAD

RICHMOND

PARK

HOLLY
LODGE

WHITE
LODGE

PEN
PONDS

N

1 MILE

Richmond Park, East Sheen and Palewell Commons

Richmond Park is one of the Royal Parks but you do not have to go far into it to appreciate how different it is from the inner-London parks. There are 2,500 acres of rolling landscape with long views over hills and hollows, woods and meadows, streams and ponds, enclosed plantations and wide open grassland. The large herds of red and fallow deer which roam throughout the Park are one of its greatest attractions. This walk approaches the Park through one of the bordering wooded commons, and returns through another.

....

DISTANCE: 4.0 or 5.0 miles (circular).

EXTENSION: Various routes through the park.

TERRAIN: Rough grass.

REFRESHMENTS: Pubs at start and in Christ Church Road near end of walk. Public cafeteria in park Golf Club, and sometimes on Palewell and East Sheen Commons.

TRANSPORT: Buses 33, 337 and R69. South West Trains to North Sheen station then up Manor Road; South West Trains, Silverlink and District Line to Richmond station – exit from lower concourse beside the WCs to Church Road where turn right to Sheen Road, then left (0.5 mile).

TRAVELCARD ZONE: 4 (North Sheen station is Zone 3).

STARTING POINT: Black Horse Tavern, Sheen Road, Richmond.

....

Cross Queens Road and continue on the pavement in front of the Courtlands flats, then on a diagonal paved path to a gate into East Sheen Common. Through the gate, walk up the main path straight ahead to enter Richmond Park at Bog Gate.

The path ahead is now a cycle track, so take the parallel grassy path a few yards to the right of it and continue on this, ignoring crossing paths and keeping Holly Lodge and its enclosure away to the left. Keep to the left of a small pond and continue by any of the small paths beyond up to the road. Cross over the road and go ahead to the fence of Sidmouth Wood, then follow that forward. When you can see Pen Ponds below, make for a bench and take the main track down to the causeway between the ponds, but do not cross. Turn left beside the lower pond and cross to the far end of it along the edge of a small plantation. Continue ahead, keeping along the right-hand edge of another small wood, climbing to meet the road at White Lodge. White Lodge was originally built as a hunting lodge by George I in 1727 and then added to by his successors. It is now the home of the Royal Ballet School.

Follow the drive round to the right until it ends at a gate which affords a view of the garden front of the house. Follow the fence for a few more yards, then, as it bends round, leave it for a grassy track ahead between oak trees. This track continues between a wood of oaks and sweet chestnuts and the bracken-filled dip on the left which is a deer sanctuary. When this path curves left past its intermittent fence, turn right round the lower edge of the wood to a path which heads off across open grass, with sports pitches on the left, and the lodge of Roehampton Gate in view beyond the row of willows marking the line of Beverley Brook. Cross a low footbridge over a minor stream coming from Pen Ponds and follow Beverley Brook to the road, where you should turn right over the brook. *To visit the cafeteria and WCs at the Golf Club take the path half right across the grass towards the car park.* Otherwise cross the road and follow it to Roehampton Gate.

Outside the gate, turn sharp left on a path beside the high brick park wall, crossing Beverley Brook again on to Palewell Common. Continue in the same direction by the wall or along the edge of the field alongside, and follow the path through a belt of woodland to a crossing path. *For cafeteria and WCs (if open) turn right here and walk down the field.*

To shorten the walk by a mile, continue on the path ahead past tennis courts to a small circular green – originally a pond. Cross the green to Hertford Avenue beyond. This will take you to Upper Richmond Road and buses (4.0 miles).

To continue the walk, turn left into Clare Lawn Avenue and go down Stonehill Road to Sheen Lane. Cross over, turn right and follow the curve, then turn left into Wayside to cut the corner into Christ Church Road, where you should turn left. Glance down the narrow Well Lane before passing The Plough pub and the picturesque cottages beyond, noting also Percy Lodge, built in 1740, opposite. Where Christ Church Road bends right, bear left into Fife Road and re-enter East Sheen Common. Refreshment pavilion ahead. Take the main path on the right through woodland, forking right where it crosses a small brook, and continue to the gate where you first entered the common, and back to the starting point.

EXTENSION

Many paths meet at Pen Ponds, so it is easy to add an extra loop to this walk – there are maps at all the gates. *See also suggestions at the end of Walk 7.* Bus routes which pass near five of the park gates make possible any number of long or short excursions into and across the park. A twilight walk is particularly delightful. The park remains open to pedestrians, though not vehicles, after dusk, except for one brief period during the year when deer are culled. Notice of this is displayed at the gates.

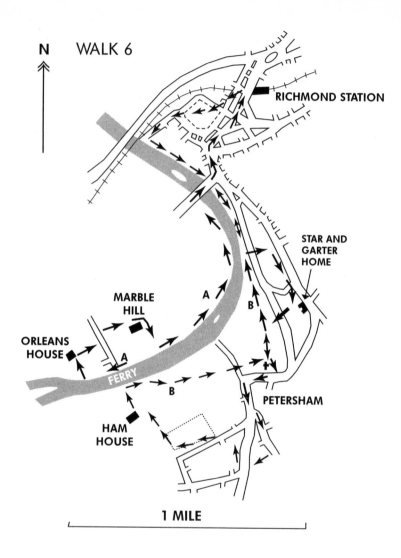

N   WALK 6

RICHMOND STATION

STAR AND
GARTER
HOME

MARBLE
HILL

A

B

ORLEANS
HOUSE

A

FERRY

B

PETERSHAM

HAM
HOUSE

1 MILE

Richmond Riverside, Petersham and Marble Hill Park

Many people admiring the view from Richmond Hill have been attracted by the pastoral nature of Petersham Meadows below. But few realise that Petersham village is a lovely mix of grand 18th- and 19th-century mansions and picturesque cottages, surrounded by fields, meadows, copse and common. This walk combines the best of Richmond's riverside with a wander through Petersham and its rural hinterland. There is the option of crossing the Thames, on one of its few remaining ferries, and returning to Richmond through Marble Hill Park on the further bank, or of returning by an alternative route on the Surrey side.

....

DISTANCE: 4.5 miles (circular). Connection with Walk 7 at Ham House.
TERRAIN: Mixed. Some of the grass and earthen paths can be very wet.
REFRESHMENTS: Pubs in Petersham, tearoom in Ham

House gardens (NT) and Marble Hill Park, refreshment facilities of all kinds in Richmond.

TRANSPORT: District Line, South West Trains and Silverlink. Buses 65, 190, 290, 371, 485, 490, H22, H37, R68, R70. Also 33, 337, R69 nearby.

TRAVELCARD ZONE: 4

STARTING POINT: Richmond station.

....

From Richmond station, cross the Quadrant by the pedestrian crossing to the left and turn back a few yards to take a path under an archway into Parkshot. Turn left to Little Green. Take a diagonal path across Little Green and the further Green beyond, forking left to go through the Tudor gateway, one of the few remains of Richmond Palace. Pass the Old Wardrobe and Trumpeter's House, exit into Old Palace Lane and turn left down to the river. Turn left again, passing the terraces of the modern riverside development, walk under Richmond Bridge and continue along the riverside promenade. When the promenade path bends leftwards up to the road, continue a few yards further through the gardens to enter a grotto-like entrance to a subway under the busy road. Climb steps on the left into Terrace Gardens and follow the path leftwards, passing the conservatory, bending left again in a gentle sweep, uphill to a thatched shelter, then up steps to a viewpoint in front of a pond with statuary. Behind the pond, take a path to the right up to a broad track and follow this up more steps to Richmond Hill Terrace with its famous view of the Thames below. Continue along the Terrace walk. Beyond, just past Wick House, turn down a path to the left of a noticeboard, dropping gently to the back of the Star and Garter Home. Fork right behind the house and at the next main path junction turn sharp right and follow this path downhill through the woods of Petersham Common to reach the road beside the Rose of York pub. Cross over to a kissing gate and take the path half left across Petersham Meadows, a totally rural landscape, to a metal zig-zag. Follow the hedged path leading past farm fields to St Peter's Church.

The church dates from the 13th century and has a fine 18th-century interior with a gallery and box pews. (If locked, a notice on the door indicates where to obtain a key.) The explorer Vancouver is buried in the churchyard. Turn back a few yards to take a narrow path between the churchyard wall and the farm, following it round bends to the road beside The Dysarts pub, opposite a pedestrian gate into Richmond Park. (WCs through gate.) Turn right past the pub following the narrow pavement past a series of magnificent 17th- and 18th-century houses and the ornate archway which leads to the East driveway to Ham House. Opposite, between the old forge and the Fox and Duck pub, is the Watchman's Box and Village Lockup of 1782. Cross at the traffic lights and turn up Sudbrook Lane, passing some of the more modest houses and cottages, which are as typical of Petersham as its grand mansions. (Dickens rented a cottage here on more than one occasion.) Bute Avenue on the left leads to All Saints Church, ornate in red brick and terracotta, now redundant but well worth a couple of minutes' diversion. Continue up Sudbrook Lane to the white archway of Sudbrook Park, now a golf clubhouse, built in 1726 by James Gibbs for the Duke of Argyll and Greenwich.

From the archway, turn down Hazel Lane to the road and cross over to a back alley to the right of the corner house opposite. This soon opens out and passes a terrace of pretty cottages. Turn left at the end, passing a school, to the Copse. Your general direction is diagonally across this area of grass, bushes and trees. There are plenty of paths, but the bridleways can be deep in mud. So, from the corner of the school fence, take the path across the grass to the left. At a crossing path coming from wooden fences, continue ahead for a few yards and then bend left on a path between brambles and oaks heading towards open grass. Turn right on a crossing path coming from houses on the left, finally joining a bridleway to reach the corner of the garden wall of Ham House. Walk down the broad track with the wall on the left and polo ground on the right and follow the wall round to the entrance to Ham House and its gardens. *Connection with Walk 7.*

In dry weather you can cross the grass in front of the gates to reach the river towpath, where turn right to the ferry steps. If the ground is wet, turn back a few yards to take a path half left across the grass to a corner where two fences meet, and turn left over a concrete causeway to the towpath and ferry steps. (Note that a stile at this corner also gives access to a path across a couple of fields. This provides an alternative route for Option B (below) when the towpath is flooded at very high tides.)

You now have the option of crossing by ferry to return by the Middlesex bank (Option A) or by the Surrey bank (Option B). The ferry runs daily between March and October, and at weekends only between November and February.

Option A. From the ferry steps, hail the ferryman at Hammerton's boatyard opposite. On alighting at the opposite side, turn left and continue along the river on the tarmac path through the riverside gardens, following the path round to cross a road and enter by a pedestrian gate the grounds of Orleans House. The elegant Octagon Room ahead, another James Gibbs design, is all that is left of Orleans House, built in 1710 but taking its name from the tenancy of the exiled Duke of Orleans, later King Louis Philippe. Alongside it is the Orleans House Gallery. From the Octagon, cross the drive and continue past a lamppost on a broad path through a small wood to exit into Orleans Road. Turn left for a few yards to a gate into Marble Hill Park. (A short diversion up Orleans and Chapel Roads into Montpelier Row brings you to one of the most elegant terraces in Twickenham, and there is another entrance into the Park from the main road beyond.) In the Park, walk ahead past the coach-house (cafe and WCs) and pass the entrance to Marble Hill House. Just beyond the house, turn down a narrow fenced path round to the river frontage of this delightful Palladian villa. Cross the lawn, curving left along the shrubbery fence to the Grotto, then follow the broad tarmac path rightwards, past the ancient Black Walnut tree, out of the Park. Turn left along the riverside walk, with splendid views across to Richmond Hill, back to the bridge. Climb up steps to cross the bridge and return through the town.

Option B. If not crossing by the ferry, continue in the Richmond direction for 100 yards or so, then at a public footpath sign cross a low concrete wall and wooden footbridge over a ditch. Continue on the path ahead (*the high-tide escape route joins at a stile on the right*), alongside the playing fields of the German School. Cross a broad track to a high-fenced path opposite, emerging in River Lane next to Petersham Lodge – another fine house, built in 1740. Cross over to a walled alley opposite which leads back to the farm and church. Retrace your outward journey along the hedged path as far as the metal zig-zag, but take the main path straight ahead across the Meadows and out through a kissing gate to the riverside gardens (WCs on the right). Continue through the gardens and under Richmond Bridge as far as Water Lane where you should turn up to George Street and go through the town back to the station and buses.

HAMMERTON'S FERRY:

Tel. 020 8892 9620.

Runs daily, March–Oct; weekends only Nov–Feb.

Charge: 40p.

HAM HOUSE (NT):

Open April–Oct (daily); closed Thurs and Fri 1p.m.–5p.m.

Gardens open daily; closed Thurs and Fri 10.30a.m.–6p.m. (or dusk if earlier). Admission charges apply.

ORLEANS HOUSE GALLERY:

Open Tues–Sat 1p.m.–5.30p.m.; Sun and bank holidays 2p.m.–5.30p.m. (4.30p.m. Oct–March). Entrance: free.

MARBLE HILL HOUSE (English Heritage):

Open April–Sep (daily) 10a.m.–6p.m.;

Oct–March (Wed–Sun) 10a.m.–4p.m.

Admission charges apply.

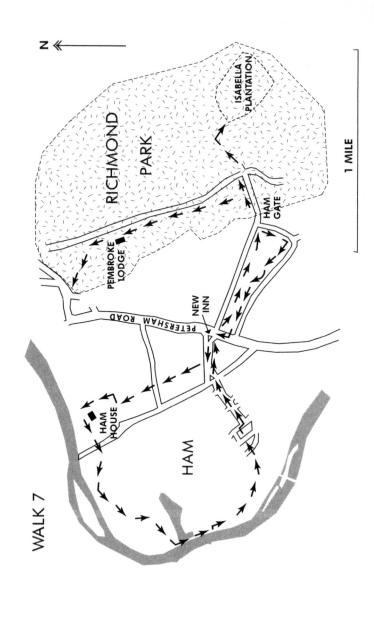

WALK 7

RICHMOND PARK

ISABELLA PLANTATION

PEMBROKE LODGE

HAM GATE

NEW INN

PETERSHAM ROAD

HAM HOUSE

HAM

N

1 MILE

Ham Common and Riverside Lands

A short walk but one which plunges you into a wilderness far removed from London and its suburbs. After the placid village green where we start – with a pub at each corner and a willow-fringed pond – followed by the formal grandeur of Ham House and its gardens, the sheer wildness of Ham Riverside Lands comes as a surprise. It is a bewildering area with few landmarks, paths disappearing into thickets and the Thames curving round it in a great loop. Yet the richness and variety of its wildlife is enchanting – look out for orchids in early summer, and it's great for blackberries later in the year.

....

DISTANCE: 3.0 miles (circular). Connection with Walk 6 at Ham House.

EXTENSION: To Ham Gate and back (1.5 miles). Further extensions within Richmond Park (1.5 and 2.0 miles).

TERRAIN: Rough paths throughout.

REFRESHMENTS: Pubs at Ham Common. Tearoom in

Ham House gardens (NT) and at Pembroke Lodge on the first extension within Richmond Park.

TRANSPORT: Bus 65 from Richmond station (District Line, South West Trains and Silverlink) or from Kingston station (South West Trains).

TRAVELCARD ZONE: 4 for Richmond, 6 for Kingston.

STARTING POINT: New Inn, Petersham Road, Ham Common.

....

Pass the front of the New Inn and continue along the right-hand edge of the open stretch of Ham Common. Past a convent turn right through white gates between two lodges and walk up the long drive known as Melancholy Walk towards the south front of Ham House, crossing over a road. At the garden gates, turn briefly right, go left on a path between the garden wall and a polo ground, following the wall round to pass the main entrance to house and gardens. Ham House is an outstanding house of the Jacobean period, with 17th-century furniture, paintings and textiles and contemporary gardens.

Continue past the house and cross over a drive to a playing field. Cross this diagonally to the far right corner and go through wooden barriers facing you on to a broad hedged track which emerges eventually through similar barriers on to an open space, with noticeboards visible to the right.

Turn left on the bridleway, skirting woodland with

open scrubby grassland on the right. This bridleway leads to the Thames Young Mariners Basin, but can be very muddy and churned up so leave it after about 100 yards (just before a rough wooden seat between two narrow paths into the woodland) for a path half right. Fork right again on another broad path and keep in this direction (south-west) across open grass towards distant trees. Past a low iron marker, the path reaches the point where the fence of the Young Mariners Basin meets the river towpath. (It is worth remembering in this wild area criss-crossed with paths that the fence and the towpath will both lead you to this point.)

Cross over the entrance to the Basin and continue on the towpath beyond the Basin itself. Take the first clear, wide path up the low bank to meet a broad gravel track above the towpath, and turn right. This track curves away from the river among a multitude of bushes and wild flowers. After crossing over another track, the track eventually joins the surfaced driveway up from Teddington Lock, near houses.

Turn left along this, cross Riverside Drive and follow the cycleway signs up a couple of alleyways and up Lock Road, back to Ham Common at the pond. There are elegant houses and pretty cottages on both sides of the green and on some turnings off it, notably Ham Street and Ham Gate Avenue.

EXTENSION: TO HAM GATE AND BACK (1.5 MILES)

From New Inn, cross the main road at the pedestrian crossing and take the horse track opposite. This can be followed all the way to Ham Gate, but a surface provided for horses can be heavy going for walkers, so follow it for 50 yards or so only, ignoring the first path off it but taking the second one half-right soon after a bend. Follow this up the right-hand edge of a meadow with riding circles – it may be necessary to swerve briefly into the woods to get round a fence – then bear right after the last circle into the woods. Turn left when you meet a crossing track and follow this through the woods for 200 yards. When this path forks each side of a tiny triangle of grass with a silver birch tree on it, take the left fork which eventually rejoins the main horse track, and continue in the same direction to the junction of Ham Gate Avenue with Church Road. Ham Gate into Richmond Park is just past white-painted Park Gate House (WCs inside the gate). *For suggestions for short walks within the Park from this point, see the next two Extensions.*

To return to the New Inn, turn right and walk down the path alongside Church Road to the corner with Latchmere Lane. Leave the road here to turn right on a broad track which continues through the woodland causewayed on a low bank, eventually approaching Church Road again. A crossing path starts from the road between two large horse chestnut trees. Turn right on this path, which is intermittently edged with logs, and follow it to a crossing track. The logs continue to the right, but turn left on a narrower path between brambles. Continue in the same general direction, keeping on the main path just to the left of any open grassy area until it brings you out on to the Upper Ham Road, 100 yards from the New Inn.

Woodland paths are notoriously hard to follow, but this strip of woodland is quite narrow. If in doubt, bear left rather than right and at worst you will come out on one of the roads either side, which are usually quiet and quite pleasant to walk down.

EXTENSION: TO PEMBROKE LODGE AND PETERSHAM (1.5 MILES)

From the pond in the park beyond Ham Gate, take either of the two steep paths up the bank beyond, and turn left along the ridge path at the top with its fine views. Approaching a fence, go through metal gates into the gardens of Pembroke Lodge. There is a cafeteria in Pembroke Lodge, WCs and sometimes an ice-cream kiosk in the car park to the right. Continue beyond the fine Lodge and gardens to the Henry VIII Mound, worth climbing for its surprise view to the City as well as into Surrey. A gate out of the gardens beneath the Mound leads to a path which takes you downhill to the Petersham gate opposite The Dysarts pub, where the 65 bus will return you to your starting point.

EXTENSION LOOP: TO ISABELLA PLANTATION AND
BACK (2.0 MILES)

Ham Gate is only 0.6 mile from Isabella Plantation –
lovely at any time but particularly so in the spring when
azaleas provide banks of colour. To reach the Plantation,
follow one of the paths beside the road from Ham Gate
to the crossroads, then walk along the road opposite
(which is closed to traffic) to the drive on the right,
signposted to the Woodland Garden. A map inside the
enclosure will help you to plan a tour. Return to Ham
Gate to complete the walk back to the New Inn.

HAM HOUSE:
For opening hours see Walk 6.

Osterley Park, Heston Common and Norwood Green

Osterley Park is enhanced by its lovely setting, described by Pevsner as a 'forgotten fragment of countryside'. A visit to the house and Park is always a pleasure, but it is the surrounding farm fields, common grazing land, the village greens of Norwood Green and Wyke Green plus (on the Extension) the ancient woodland of Long Wood, which make this walk a country experience.

....

DISTANCE: 3.5 or 4 miles (circular). Connection with Walk 9 at Hanwell on Extension.
EXTENSION: To Grand Union Canal (3.0 miles).
TERRAIN: Mixed, some rough field paths.
REFRESHMENTS: Pub and cafe at Norwood Green, cafeteria in Osterley Park (when house is open), pub at Hanwell Lock on Extension.
TRANSPORT: Piccadilly Line. Bus H91.
TRAVELCARD ZONE: 4
STARTING POINT: Osterley station.

WALK 8

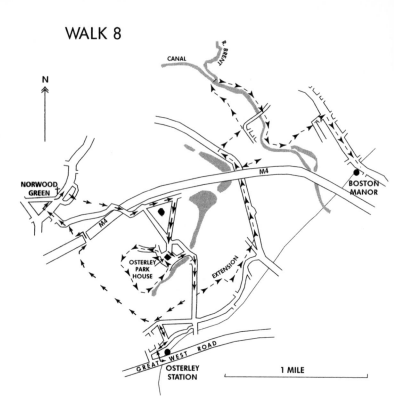

N

CANAL
R. BRENT

M4

NORWOOD
GREEN

M4

BOSTON
MANOR

OSTERLEY
PARK
HOUSE

EXTENSION

GREAT WEST ROAD

OSTERLEY
STATION

1 MILE

Turn right out of the station and right again along an alleyway into Bassett Gardens, where turn right then left. Cross Jersey Road to enter Osterley Park through an open gateway in the wall. Turn left on a path along the edge of a field. Beyond a hedge, turn right on a path through trees and you are soon walking along the edge of Heston Common where tethered horses graze and the tower of Heston Church is just visible in trees on the far side. The path continues in and out of strips of woodland but keeps near the hedge until it leads between fences to a high pedestrian bridge over the M4, providing a view of the farm fields of Osterley. Follow the path on the far side along the right-hand edge of a field to a gate into Osterley Lane and turn left.

At Norwood Green, turn right along the edge of the Green. Continue down Tentelow Lane, past the brick and flint church. It is worth going a little further to see the 1767 school building with its Gothic windows – and there may be a cafe open beyond – but turn down the further side of The Plough and along an alleyway, which leads out to a path across the middle of a field, and up on to Osterley Lane again where it crosses the M4.

The lane curves round to a couple of lodges, but continues ahead, beyond a gate, as a broad sandy track. Go down this track then turn through a wooden gate beside another lodge into the park. Follow the drive and go through a gate towards the house. (WCs on the right and cafeteria in the Elizabethan stables beyond.)

Osterley House and Park belong to the National

Trust. The Park and gardens provide free access to the public until 7.30 p.m., or sunset if earlier. Opening hours of the house are given at the end. The house was built by Sir Thomas Gresham in 1575 but its present classical exterior and delicate interior decoration are due to Robert Adam's alterations between 1760 and 1780. Walk down the side of the house to view the garden front.

If time allows, to visit the pleasure grounds turn right along the path to the little semi-circular Adam Garden House then walk through the gardens to the Temple of Pan. Beyond the Temple, a path through the shrubbery takes a great sweep beyond the Great Meadow and brings you eventually to the tip of the lake which you follow back to the house (an optional extra loop of just over half a mile). *Or* kissing gates in the fence allow you to walk across the meadow with its grazing cattle for a splendid view of the back of the house.

To finish the walk, continue on the gravel drive past the main entrance front of the house, curve round between the two lakes, through a gate and down the road. Shortly after passing the farm shop on the left, two kissing gates face each other across the drive. *For Extension see below.* The one on the right just past a house gives entry to a fenced path which leads back between fields to the gateway in the wall where you first entered the park. Retrace your steps to the station.

EXTENSION: TO GRAND UNION CANAL AND
CONNECTIONS WITH WALKS 9 AND 10

Beyond the farm shop, go through the left-hand kissing gate and follow the fenced path through farm fields, round a dog-leg and out of the park on to Wyke Green. Follow the park fence, crossing the drive in front of two lodges, and continue to curve round the edge of the Green, coming out on Windmill Lane opposite the Hare and Hounds pub. Cross the road and turn left.

Shortly after passing under the M4 you will see on the right a footpath signpost pointing through wooden fences to a very tempting path through Long Wood (worth a diversion). The Brent River and Canal Society hope eventually to link the further end of the wood, beyond which runs a freight railway line, with a crossing over the railway by means of a path beneath a raised field. Until this happens it is necessary to continue along the road for another three or four minutes. Just beyond a gate into the riding school, go through a kissing gate on to a fenced path leading to the board crossing over the railway line (which now only serves a waste disposal plant).

Trumpers Way, facing you, leads straight to the canal, but a metal gate on the left leads into Trumpers Field on a recently created path which soon opens out into a wide, rough field with a couple of benches. Through a gate at the far end of the field turn right down to the Hanwell Flight of Locks. Cross on the lock gate of the lowest one. *You are now on the route of Walk 9.* The Flight of Locks and Three Bridges are on your left. The Fox pub is in Green Lane just beyond the humpback bridge over the Brent to your right.

To finish the walk, turn right over the humpback bridge and along the towpath for nearly a mile to the weir before Osterley Lock. Climb up to the playing fields, cross them half right to an exit leading to Boston Road where you should turn right for Boston Manor Piccadilly Line station.

OSTERLEY HOUSE (NT):

Open April–Oct (Wed–Sun and bank holidays) 1p.m.– 4.30p.m.

Show your Travelcard for £1 discount off admission charge. NT members can claim £1 voucher towards cost of guidebook or cream tea.

Brentford to Hanwell by canal and Boston Manor Park

This walk starts in the most architecturally distinguished part of Brentford, The Butts, then sets off up the canal. The River Brent which rises on Moat Mount just to the north of London is 'captured' by the Grand Union Canal from Hanwell down to the Thames. A couple of loops have been left uncanalised, and our route uses these stretches as a contrast to the canal, where there are interesting reminders of the industrial past, but whose environment is now predominantly green.

....

DISTANCE: 4.5 miles (linear). Connections with Walk 4 at Brentford High Street and Walk 8 Extension at Trumpers Bridge or Hanwell Lock. Walk 10 continues from the end of this walk.

TERRAIN: Mostly level gravel paths.

REFRESHMENTS: Pubs and cafes in Brentford. Pubs in Hanwell.

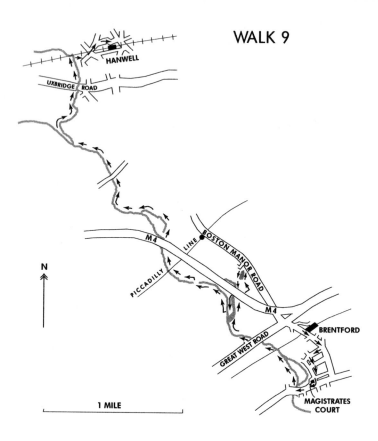

WALK 9

HANWELL

UXBRIDGE ROAD

N

M4

PICCADILLY

LINE

BOSTON MANOR ROAD

M4

GREAT WEST ROAD

BRENTFORD

MAGISTRATES
COURT

1 MILE

TRANSPORT: South West Trains. Bus E8 to station, E2 nearby. Buses 235, 237, 267, H29 (Mon–Sat) for alternative starting point. Note that Hanwell station at the end has no Sunday service.
TRAVELCARD ZONE: 4
STARTING POINT: Brentford station.
ALTERNATIVE STARTING POINT: Magistrates Court, Brentford High Street.

....

Go up the approach road or steps on to Boston Manor Road and turn left. Cross the road and turn right down Somerset Road opposite the Public Library, then first left into The Butts, a fine square of houses dating from the 1690s up to the 18th century and the scene of boisterous fairs and riotous Middlesex elections. Cross to the far right corner. The building on the right-hand side was originally a Canal Boatmen's Institute. Beyond this, go down the passageway, pass the Magistrates Court, *the alternative starting point,* and turn right along the High Street to the canal bridge. Cross the bridge, go down steps on the right on to the canal towpath, alongside the Brentford Gauging Locks and Freight Depot. This section of the Grand Junction Canal was opened in 1794 and the Depot developed as a busy transhipment centre where goods from the London docks were transferred on and off Thames barges. The small brick building on the lockside was the toll office. Cross over the swing bridge, round a vast canopied

71

warehouse, under the railway and the Great West Road to a graceful wooden footbridge. Cross this and enter Boston Manor Park. Turn left round the playing field, then continue following the fence with glimpses of the Brent through it. Turn up a broad, grassy path under the M4 flyover to the lawn behind Boston Manor. Go round to look at the front of this fine Jacobean house, then return and walk forward to the lake (WCs here).

Continue ahead to circle the lake. Near the end of the circuit, steps on the right with a Nature Trail signpost lead down to an uncanalised loop of the Brent. Follow the Nature Trail path back to the flyover where you should turn right through the gates, cross the bridge over the river and drop down to a path on the left, following it to Clitheroe's Lock. Cross the lock gates back on to the towpath, turn right and continue up it, re-crossing the canal at Gallows Bridge. After going under the Piccadilly Line and then the M4, a path turns up beside another loop of the river, glimpses of its swampy, tangled banks providing an interesting alternative to the canal towpath. At the top, the path turns left above this area of scrub along the edge of a playing field. At the far corner you can take a wide path which drops back down to the towpath just beyond Osterley Lock and Weir, or you can keep on one of the paths at a higher level as far as Trumpers Bridge. Continue on the towpath beyond to the point where river and canal finally part company. The Fox pub is round the corner on Green Lane. An old bridge carries the towpath over the Brent, and ahead is the first of the Hanwell Flight of Locks. *Walk 8 joins here.* The towpath climbs the flight of six locks, which raise the canal 53 feet in 0.3 mile, and continues past the intersection known as Three Bridges, where the road crosses over the canal and the railway line is far beneath. *We meet the same canal further on in Walks 17, 24 and 25.*

However, our route leaves the canal between the first and second locks, where a footpath waymark points down steps to a path which follows the river underneath the Uxbridge Road at Hanwell. To finish the walk here, go up steps on the far side for buses to Ealing Broadway. For Hanwell station (Thames Trains to Ealing Broadway and Paddington, Mon–Sat) continue along the river towards the dramatic arches of the Wharncliffe Viaduct and cross the river by the footbridge. *For Walk 10, turn left from the further side of the footbridge and walk under the viaduct.* For the station, go straight ahead beside the viaduct on a path through a little wood and left on a tarmac path beyond. Turn left on the road under the railway arch, then right and right again down Campbell Road to Hanwell station.

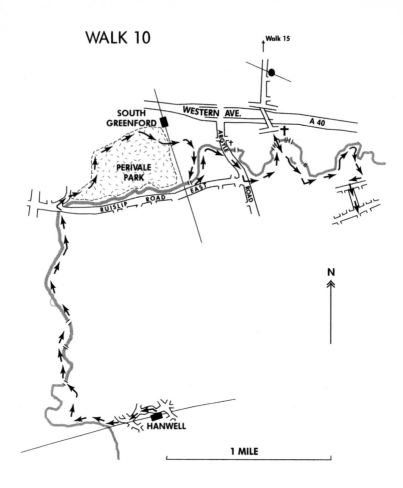

WALK 10

SOUTH GREENFORD

WESTERN AVE.

A 40

Walk 15

PERIVALE PARK

ARGYLE

ROAD

RUISLIP ROAD EAST

HANWELL

N

1 MILE

Hanwell to Perivale along the River Brent

For much of this walk we continue to follow the River Brent in its meandering course through the greener parts of Ealing. The parks of Brent Lodge, Perivale and Pitshanger, with their accompanying golf courses, provide wide areas of open space. There is abundant wildlife along the river, including giant hogweed.

....

DISTANCE: 4.0 miles (linear). Connections with Walk 9 at the start and Walk 15 near the end.

TERRAIN: Level, mostly grass paths.

REFRESHMENTS: Cafeterias in Brent Lodge Park, Perivale Park and Gurnell Leisure Centre. Pub on A40 on the route to Perivale station.

TRANSPORT: Thames Trains to Hanwell station (no Sunday service). Bus E3. Buses 83, 207, 607, E4 (E3, E8 nearby) to Brent Bridge, Uxbridge Road, Hanwell. To start at this point, follow directions in last paragraph of Walk 9.

TRAVELCARD ZONE: 4
STARTING POINT: Hanwell station.

....

From Hanwell station, turn left along Campbell Road and left along Golden Manor. Turn right immediately before the bridge and take the path alongside the railway embankment, waymarked Brent River Park Footpath. After 50 yards, turn left to meet the path coming up from under the viaduct *where Walk 9 and the path from the buses connect.* Do not go under the viaduct but continue straight ahead on the path alongside the River Brent (waymarked Brent River Park Walk and West London Waterway Walks). After passing through the gate at the bottom of the hedge, the waymarked route continues up some steps and along the river. At this point, leave the waymarked route and follow the tarmac path up towards Brent Lodge. Here you will find the cafeteria, WCs and a collection of animals (the park is known locally as Bunny Park). Regain the riverside either by going across the grass to the left of the aviaries and down the slope (watch out for pitch and putt) or by making for the church and turning left down the steps alongside it.

At the bottom, cross the Brent by Boles Bridge and turn right. Either follow the waymarks to cross the Brent again by a footbridge beyond the golf course, or follow paths along the river on either side until you come once again to the waymarked path. Beyond the golf course, a grassy path continues on the right-hand bank. At a low concrete structure, steps up the bank lead to a higher route with a good view ahead of Horsenden Hill. Return to the riverside path at the end of the field and continue to Ruislip Road.

Across the road to the right, the BRP waymark points down a path winding beside the river – an attractive path but close to the road. For a quieter route, turn left over the river bridge, right down Costons Lane and right again past a BRP noticeboard into Perivale Park. Walk along the path, cross the footbridge and follow the stream leftwards along a grassy ridge. Turn right in front of a line of Balsam Poplar trees by a ditch. Follow the path to the right of the tennis courts and fenced athletics track towards an arch in the railway viaduct (public cafe with WCs in clubhouse on right). Go underneath the viaduct (which carries the local line between Ealing Broadway and Greenford) and along Stockdove Way beside a field fence. Enter the field by the stile at the far end and walk down the left-hand side beside the Brent. Continue across the next field to an opening in the fence near the far right-hand corner and go up steps to a track below the railway embankment. Turn left on the track towards the road and, immediately after crossing the river, turn left on a path beside it, to rejoin the waymarked route. Continue along the path, between brambles and giant hogweed, to a field behind the giant Gurnell Leisure Centre and swimming pool (entrance to cafeteria, bar and WCs on far side by road). Follow the path along the edge of the field until you reach Argyle Road, where you should turn right.

Cross over Argyle Road at the next junction to reach the waymarked path and cycle track opposite. Stay on this tarmac path, through a golf course, forking left at the next two path junctions. Shortly after the second fork, cross a footbridge over the Brent and continue up to where the little, weatherboarded, 16th-century tower of Perivale Church appears on the right.

To return from Perivale Central Line station or to connect with Walk 15, continue past the church and the lychgate, go down Old Church Lane (opposite) to a pedestrian bridge over Western Avenue (A40) and continue up Horsenden Lane South to the station, or to the canal bridge beyond.

To visit Pitshanger Park and finish on bus routes, return over the footbridge but go straight ahead at the next path junction. At the end of this path, turn left into Pitshanger Park and follow the river round this little park to leave it by the ornamental gates into Meadvale Road. Walk up Barnsfield Road to Pitshanger Lane for E2 or E9 buses to Ealing Broadway or Brentford.

Wimbledon Common, Putney Heath and Cannizaro Park

Roehampton and Wimbledon lie on either side of Putney Heath and Wimbledon Common, which together form one of the largest areas of rough heathland left within Greater London, open to the public. There are bus routes on three sides, so it is not difficult to reach. Yet it remains a mysterious place which you can return to again and again and each time find new places. This walk keeps to the more open, eastern half of the heathland where the windmill is a useful landmark. Cannizaro Park is a delightful contrast to the wilderness of the heath: lawns, flowerbeds, exotic trees and great banks of shrubs, with a central formal garden that is a fine backdrop to opera on summer evenings. The hilltop villages of Roehampton and Wimbledon are also well worth exploring.

....

DISTANCE: 3.0 miles returning by bus from Wimbledon; 5.5 miles (circular) back to Roehampton.

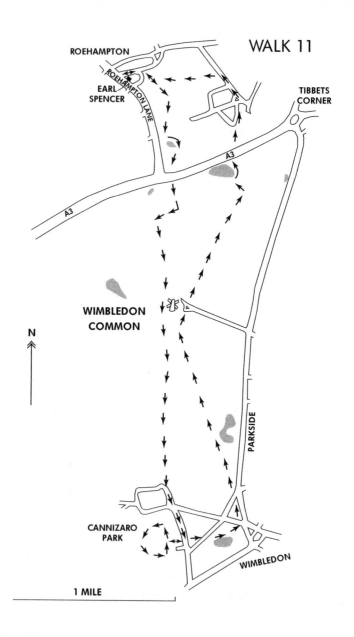

WALK 11

ROEHAMPTON

EARL
SPENCER

ROEHAMPTON LANE

TIBBETS
CORNER

A3

A3

WIMBLEDON
COMMON

N

PARKSIDE

CANNIZARO
PARK

WIMBLEDON

1 MILE

EXTENSION: Various routes through Wimbledon Common and Putney Heath.

TERRAIN: Rough paths throughout.

REFRESHMENTS: Pubs in Roehampton and Wimbledon villages, cafes in Wimbledon village. Cafeteria at the Windmill, hotel restaurant in Cannizaro Park.

TRANSPORT: Buses 72, 74, 85, 170, 265, 485 (Mon–Sat). Nearest stations are Barnes, Putney (South West Trains), Putney Bridge (District Line), all with bus connections.

TRAVELCARD ZONE: 3

STARTING POINT: Earl Spencer pub, Roehampton.

....

From the ornamental fountain in the centre of the village, walk to the left of the Earl Spencer pub and go up Medfield Street to the end of the houses on the right. Take a path half right across the grass to join a broad track. On the track, turn right, fork right almost at once past a cycle/bridleway post, then continue to Scio Pond. Turn left to go round two sides of the pond and continue ahead into the trees and through a subway under the A3.

Beyond the subway, continue on the main track for a couple of hundred yards until, past some hillocks, you come to a junction of paths in a clearing. Take the second path on the right, heading into a tunnel of trees and emerging into the open just before a stone memorial to the Tangier Regiment.

Climb the hillock on your left and keep on top for the long view south and west with the windmill appearing ahead among the trees. In spite of their thick covering these hillocks are not a natural feature. They are formed from soil excavated in the 1960s for the Tibbets Corner road improvements. Keep on ahead and drop down, from the far side, on to a faint path (half right) heading into woods. Bear left at the second crossing path and continue to the car park in front of the windmill (cafeteria, WCs and Windmill Museum).

Facing the cafeteria, follow the fence round to the right and pass the golf clubhouse. Below you is a thickly wooded hillside with Queen's Mere in its depths. From the corner of the fence beyond the clubhouse, continue ahead on a broad path across grass, cross the wide track and adjacent horse track and continue for another half-mile through an open area of grass and heather, dotted with trees and lined by thin woodland, until you reach houses at the corner of two roads. Keep ahead on the common to the left of West Place, cross Camp Road (Fox and Grapes pub a few yards down), cross to the path alongside the houses of West Side Common and turn in through the high, brick gateposts of Cannizaro Park.

In the park, follow the drive to a crossing path coming from the house (now a hotel) and turn right past a small white aviary to an open lawn (WCs ahead on right). From the lawn, follow a gravel path leftwards to a pond, then continue through the walled gardens –

if closed during open air performance season circle them to the right – to the far end of the lawn beyond and cross a little stone bridge. You can wander many ways through the shrubbery and woodland, but to see the best of them turn left up shallow steps then zig-zag right and left up more steps to a viewpoint above great banks of azaleas, ablaze with colour in the spring. Continue uphill to emerge finally by any path on to the wide lawn in front of the house. The formal beds to the right of the house are also open to the public.

Leave the park by the gate you came in, take the path ahead across the grass to a road, cross towards a pond and bear left towards the war memorial, half hidden by a tree.

Beyond lies the old hilltop village of Wimbledon, not to be confused with the modern suburb which developed around the station a long way down the hill. It is an attractive place with some old-style cottages, pleasant cafes and old pubs, and shops that are ideal for browsing in. A gate lodge and well house near the church are all that remain of Wimbledon's grand manor houses. The famous Lawn Tennis Club is a little further down Church Road.

To finish the walk here, go to the left of the war memorial to the bus stop for bus 93 to Putney (change at the Green Man to return to Roehampton) or cross the road for bus 93 down to Wimbledon station (South West Trains and District Line).

To continue the walk back to Roehampton, keep left,

still on the common, past the war memorial. Take a path between a horse track and the road, passing behind the bus shelter, cross Cannizaro Road and go down a horse track for a few yards, then fork left on to a path with No Cycling posts and follow the path for the best part of a mile, nearly back to the windmill. Turn right on one of the paths before the buildings, pass the large iron mill contraption, and cross the road. Take the path ahead, but when it divides almost at once into three, take the middle path with a No Cycling post. After 0.3 mile, across an open area of grass and heather dotted with birch trees, the path enters a wooded belt. Take the first path on the left over a tiny ditch through the trees towards King's Mere and the sound of the A3 traffic. Follow the path rightwards along the lake, then left round its head towards the A3 and go down the subway. Go up the tarmac path on the further side, then right on the earthen path and continue beside a road to Telegraph Road (Telegraph pub on right). Turn left, cross Portsmouth Road, and at the end of the block of houses opposite a cricket pitch, turn left on a path up the side of the last house and keep on this main track back to an open area, where you rejoin your outward route, bearing left to return to Roehampton.

Note that Roehampton is worth exploring to see its superb 18th-century houses. Most are now colleges, including Mount Clare, now in the improbable setting of the 1950s Alton Estate. The centre building of Queen

Mary's Hospital behind its grand gates is the 18th-century Roehampton House.

EXTENSION

Days can be spent exploring Wimbledon Common and Putney Heath. Walks can be extended by taking any path dropping westward from the central plateau through the woods to Beverley Brook, which runs along its westward edge, and following that north, crossing the A3 by the high pedestrian bridge, to enter Richmond Park at Robin Hood Gate.

WINDMILL MUSEUM:
Open Easter to end Oct (weekends and
bank holidays) 2p.m.–5p.m.
Tel: 202 8947 2825.

WALK 12

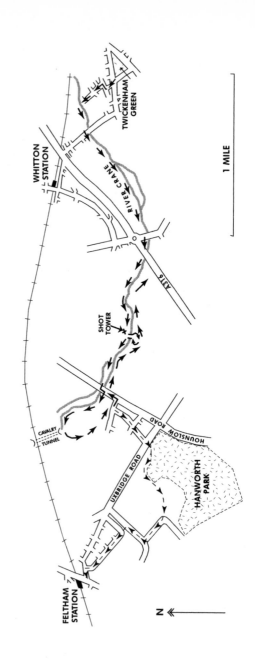

FELTHAM STATION

WHITTON STATION

TWICKENHAM GREEN

RIVER CRANE

SHOT TOWER

CAVALRY TUNNEL

UXBRIDGE ROAD

HOUNSLOW ROAD

HANWORTH PARK

A316

N

1 MILE

Along the River Crane

A wide strip of woodland and meadow grassland with a river running through, a millstream rushing over a weir to join it, an island nature reserve in the middle – what could be more peaceful? Yet this was the site of gunpowder mills up until 1926. You can look out for the signs of this industry, such as the millstones near the Shot Tower and the waterwheel channel you cross to the island, or you can simply enjoy the peace and quiet of this little-known river park.

....

DISTANCE: 2.5 or 3.25 miles (linear); 4.25 or 5.0 miles (circular) from Whitton station.

EXTENSION: Across Hanworth Park to Feltham (1.7 miles). From Twickenham Green (linear, 4.25 or 5.0 miles).

TERRAIN: Mostly good grass or earthen paths, though the Cavalry Tunnel loop is rougher. Not recommended in very wet conditions as the riverside path can be flooded in places.

REFRESHMENTS: Pubs on Twickenham Green and Hanworth Road. Also at end of Feltham Extension.
TRANSPORT: Buses 110, 267, 281, 290, 490, H22, R70. South West Trains to Whitton station. Turn left and left again down Jubilee Avenue, cross A316 by subway, down Meadway to start of Crane Park.
TRAVELCARD ZONE: 4 for buses, 5 for Whitton station, 6 for Feltham station on Extension.
STARTING POINT: Twickenham Green, corner of First Cross Road.

....

From the north-west corner of Twickenham Green, cross Staines Road and turn down Briar Road between the pub and shops. Turn a couple of corners to continue in the same direction down Mereway Road and over the River Crane, at the point where the Duke of Northumberland's River leaves the River Crane, into Kneller Gardens. Turn left and follow the riverside path round to Meadway. Cross and enter Crane Park. *The route from Whitton station joins here.*

Follow the track ahead or walk along the river bank. Beyond Mill Road Weir you have the alternative of an earthen path on the opposite bank, returning at the next footbridge. Keep beside the river on the cycle track underneath the two busy roads, out into the further, wider section of the park. Continue along the river bank or on the higher tarmac path in muddy conditions. All paths lead to the Shot Tower.

Soon the path passes by a couple of steep little hillocks – natural tree-covered features now but originally constructed to deflect explosions from the gunpowder mills. The tall, conical, brick building you soon reach has long been known as the Shot Tower, though it was probably used as a lookout and to house pumping machinery. It is sometimes open at weekends and has displays on the natural life and industrial history of the area. Beside the Shot Tower a footbridge leads on to the Island Nature Reserve. This is open to the public and a walk round is recommended.

Continue along the river bank, over a hillock, and cross a bridge at a weir on to an island between the river and millstream, following a path through the middle of it. If too muddy, return to the surfaced path. Both paths come out on to the Hanworth/Hounslow Road either side of the millstream. *To finish the walk here* (2.5 miles), see the information about buses below, but remember you are facing in the opposite direction.

For an interesting 0.7 mile loop along to the Cavalry Tunnel and back, cross the road, turn left crossing over the Crane, and, about 30 yards ahead, turn in at a gateway signposted to Pevensey Road Nature Reserve. Follow the path (past posts with a crane waymark) down steps, across a marshy area on boardwalks (these can be slippy!) and along the left bank of the river, bending left with the river as it approaches the fences of the old Feltham Marshalling Yards. The river bends to the right and disappears next to the railed-off entrance to the

Cavalry Tunnel. From this end of the tunnel you can just see the far end where it emerges into the daylight again on Hounslow Heath. (The only way to reach Hounslow Heath from here is to go 0.7 mile up Hanworth Road, over the railway and turn up through a small recreation ground.) The path curves back beyond this point, passing a sports field fence into a more open stretch of grass, with a crematorium garden beyond the fence on the left. Continue down the middle of this grassy area to a gate leading out on to Pevensey Road near its junction with Hounslow Road. *The Extension to Hanworth Park and Feltham starts here.*

To return from here, the 111 bus passes *left* up the Hanworth Road to Hounslow or *right* up the Hounslow Road to Kingston. Or turn *right* to the traffic lights for bus 490 to Twickenham Green and Richmond; or *left* to Powder Mill Lane for a pub and bus 110 to Twickenham Green, and for bus R62 (infrequent) to Whitton for the station.

Alternatively, you can walk back along the Hanworth bank of the river to Chertsey Road (an extra mile). Cross Hounslow Road and go through a gateway on the right of the Crane (opposite the Cavalry Tunnel path). Follow the rough path beyond for a little over half a mile, passing the other side of the Nature Reserve island, with a clear view of the dipping platform at its tip. Alongside a few masonry and stone remains of a mill, a path on the right leads up to a housing estate. Ignore this, but, at any stage beyond this point, if the path beside the river is overgrown or obstructed by fallen trees, any right-hand fork will eventually lead you to the bank of a rough playing field, the far end of which borders Chertsey Road. When you reach Chertsey Road, turn left to cross the river and then left again into Hospital Bridge Road. Cross this road for buses back to Twickenham, or to walk up Percy Road to Whitton station.

EXTENSION: ACROSS HANWORTH PARK TO FELTHAM

From the gate in Pevensey Road, cross over to go down Meadow Road and continue down Woodlawn Drive. Cross Uxbridge Road and enter Hanworth Park by the Feltham Airparcs Leisure Centre (WCs in entrance hall). Take the tarmac path to the right of the driveway and fork right, cross the grass to a gate and walk up alongside the tennis courts to the open park. Turn left between the plantations of young trees towards the taller trees of a wooded enclosure. The Longford River disappears underground at this point – it was culverted when this became Hanworth Air Park. Turn right here beside an old brick blockhouse. Follow the river through a wooded strip out to a paved path beside the school sports pitches. Turn left out to a road and right down Forest Road. At the junction with Browells Lane, take the right-hand branch. Continue to the Uxbridge Road for the Airman pub and the 490 bus back to

Twickenham Green and Richmond. For Feltham station and other buses, leave Browells Lane opposite the entrance to a school sports complex, cross over to an alleyway into Danesbury Road and continue into Cardinal Road. Turn left at the top for Feltham station.

Bushy Park and Hampton Court Home Park

These are both Royal Parks and have grand avenues aligned with those in the formal gardens of Hampton Court Palace. Further away from the Palace the parkland is less formal, dotted with ponds and clumps of trees. The wooded fringe along the Longford River opposite Hampton village is a secret wilderness. Fallow deer roam both parks and Bushy also has red deer.

....

DISTANCE: 5.0 miles (circular). Connection with Walk 7 (2.0 miles from Kingston Bridge).
EXTENSION: To Hampton village (1.5 miles).
TERRAIN: Level tarmac, gravel or grass paths.
REFRESHMENTS: Pubs at Hampton Wick, Hampton village (on the Extension) and Hampton Court. Cafeteria in gardens of Hampton Court Palace. Snack bar and mobile vans in Bushy Park car parks.
TRANSPORT: South West Trains. Buses 281, 285.
TRAVELCARD ZONE: 6

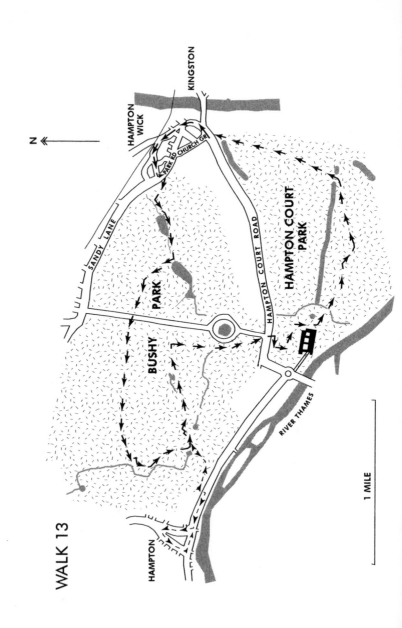

WALK 13

N ←

KINGSTON

HAMPTON WICK

PARK RD CHURCH GR

SANDY LANE

BUSHY PARK

HAMPTON COURT ROAD

HAMPTON COURT PARK

HAMPTON

RIVER THAMES

1 MILE

STARTING POINT: Hampton Wick station.
ALTERNATIVE STARTING POINT: Kingston Bridge.

....

From Hampton Wick station, turn right and cross the road to Vicarage Road opposite. At the far end, turn left into Sandy Lane and cross to enter Bushy Park at Hampton Wick Gate, beside the memorial to the shoemaker after whom Cobblers Walk is named. Maps at each gate identify the main features and amenities of the park.

From Kingston, cross Kingston Bridge. At the traffic lights just beyond the roundabout, turn up Church Grove. Opposite St John's Church, go through a gate into Church Passage, a tarmac lane between a sports field and allotments, into the park. To join the main route, bear right around two sides of a fenced cricket ground and then diagonally along a grass path, between two groups of trees to the sign-board at Hampton Wick Gate.

Inside the gate, follow Cobblers Walk, now a surfaced cycle track, as far as a bridge. Leave Cobblers Walk and keep to the left-hand side of the stream and the Leg-of-Mutton Pond. Continue along the stream until you reach the larger Heron Pond. Cross the stream here and continue straight ahead on a grassy path, through the bracken towards Hawthorn Lodge in the distance, but keeping to the right of its fence. The path crosses two grassy paths and rejoins the surfaced Cobblers Walk.

Turn left on Cobblers Walk, passing to the right of Hawthorn Lodge, and cross the road lined with over 1,000 trees which form the famous Chestnut Avenue. Carry on ahead, passing the gates of Bushy House. Cross a drive and continue ahead on Cobblers Walk, now a grassy path, keeping to the left of a car park and crossing a vast expanse of open parkland dotted with trees and grazed by red and fallow deer. It joins a surfaced track shortly before reaching a wooden gate. (Through the gate, Dukes Head Passage ahead provides a direct route to Hampton village, coming out beside the Dukes Head pub.) Go through the wooden gate, turn immediately left through another gate, then right on a somewhat vague track through the woods. Bear left when you see a low concrete pillar on the right, and continue bearing slightly left until the path reaches the Longford River. (If you walk a little way up the riverside path to the right you can look across fields to Hampton village, an astonishingly rural view.)

Leave the river and turn left to a fence and follow this past a lodge to the Woodland Gardens. There is much to see here. Continue ahead through rhododendrons, to a lake which has a waterfall at its far end. *The 1.5-mile Extension to Hampton village leaves here.* Continue beyond the waterfall, bearing left towards an open glade fringed with azaleas. Bear left then right through the azaleas, and cross a footbridge on the left opposite a pond. Walk ahead through an area of damp-loving plants, crossing two streams on the way, then turn right

BARNES POND (WALK 2)

STRAND-ON-THE-GREEN (WALK 3)

SYON HOUSE (WALK 4)

VIEW FROM RICHMOND HILL (WALK 6)

WIMBLEDON COMMON WINDMILL (WALK 11)

SHOT TOWER, CRANE PARK (WALK 12)

Key to lines

Bakerloo
Central
peak hours only
Circle
District
East London
peak hours and Sunday mornings
Hammersmith & City

Metropolitan
peak hours only
Jubilee
Northern
Piccadilly
Victoria
Waterloo & City
Docklands Light Railway

High Barnet
Totteridge & Whetstone
Woodside Park
West Finchley
Finchley Central
East Finchley
Highgate
Archway
Tufnell Park

Cockfosters
Oakwood
Southgate
Arnos Grove
Bounds Green
Wood Green
Turnpike Lane
Manor House

Kentish Town
Holloway Road
Caledonian Road

Arsenal
Finsbury Park

Tottenham Hale
Blackhorse Road
Seven Sisters
Walthamstow Central

Epping
Theydon Bois
Debden
Loughton
Buckhurst Hill

Roding Valley † Chigwell †
Grange Hill †
5
Hainault
Fairlop
Barkingside

Woodford
4
South Woodford
Snaresbrook
Wanstead
Redbridge
Newbury Park
Gants Hill
6

Upminster
Upminster Bridge
Hornchurch
Elm Park
Dagenham East
Dagenham Heathway
Becontree
Upney

ng's Cross
. Pancras
Angel
Farringdon
Barbican
Old Street
Liverpool Street
Moorgate
St. Paul's
Bank
Aldgate

Highbury & Islington

Bethnal Green
Mile End
Shoreditch †
Bow Road
Bow Church
Bromley-by-Bow
West Ham

Stratford

Barking
East Ham
Upton Park
Plaistow

Leytonstone
Leyton
3

Pudding Mill Lane

Russell Square
Chancery Lane ★
arden
† ≉ Cannon Street
ansion House
Blackfriars
Temple
nt

2
Aldgate East
Stepney Green Whitechapel
Devons Road
All Saints
East India
Shadwell Westferry
Poplar
Blackwall
Monument Tower Hill
Tower Gateway
Limehouse
Wapping West India Quay
Canary Wharf
1
Fenchurch Street
River Thames

Bus to City Airport ✈
Canning Town
Royal Victoria
Custom House
Prince Regent
Royal Albert

Beckton Park
Cyprus
Gallions Reach
Beckton

4 5 6

Rotherhithe
Canada Water
Bermondsey
Surrey Quays

Heron Quays
South Quay
Crossharbour & London Arena
Mudchute
Island Gardens

North Greenwich
for the Dome

k
London Bridge
Borough

Cutty Sark
for Maritime Greenwich
Greenwich ≉
Deptford Bridge
Elverson Road
Lewisham ≉

phant & Castle

New Cross Gate ≉
New Cross ≉

xplanation of zones

D	Station in Band D
C	Station in Band C
B	Station in Band B
A	Station in Band A · Station in Zone 6 and Band A
6	Station in Zone 6
5	Station in Zone 5
4	Station in Zone 4 · Station in both zones
3	Station in Zone 3
2	Station in Zone 2 · Station in both zones
1	Station in Zone 1 · Station in both zones

Key to symbols

O Interchange stations

≉ Connections with National Rail

🚶 Connections with National Rail within walking distance

✈ Airport interchange

★ Closed Sundays

▲ Served by Piccadilly line trains early morning and late evening

† Restricted services

Central	No service Woodford - Hainault after 2000 daily.
Circle	Cannon Street open until 1100 Mondays to Fridays. Closed Saturdays and Sundays.
District	Earl's Court - Kensington (Olympia) 0700 to 2045 Mondays to Saturdays. 0800 to 2045 Sundays.
East London	Shoreditch - Whitechapel 0700 to 1000 and 1530 to 1900 Mondays to Fridays. Closed Saturdays. Until 1500 Sundays.
Hammersmith & City	No service Whitechapel - Barking early morning or late evening Mondays to Saturdays or all day Sundays.

Northern	On Sundays between 1300 and 1730, Camden Town is open for interchange and exit only.
Piccadilly	Heathrow Terminal 4 open until 2345 Mondays to Saturdays and 2315 Sundays. No service Uxbridge - Rayners Lane early mornings and late evenings.
Waterloo & City	0615 to 2130 Mondays to Fridays. 0800 to 1830 Saturdays. Closed Sundays.

Certain stations are closed on public holidays.

BULLS BRIDGE ON THE GRAND UNION CANAL (WALK 14)

VIEW FROM HORSENDEN HILL (WALK 15)

THE RIVER CRANE (WALK 12)

HOGSMILL WALK NEAR BERRYLANDS (WALK 19)

RUISLIP LIDO (WALK 23)

to go out of the enclosure. Cross over a track and enter the next enclosure. Follow the main gravel path right through, ignoring all left-hand turns, to exit by a gate at the far right-hand corner. This is known as the Crocodile Gate because of the split log beside the footbridge.

To exit the park, follow the line of Chestnut Avenue towards the park gates beyond the Diana Fountain. For a quiet route away from the traffic, take the right-hand path of the two paths facing you. This path crosses the Longford river culvert and splits into several minor paths. Take any path leading gradually leftwards.

From the park's gates, cross the road and enter Hampton Court Palace Gardens by Lion Gate. For a short tour of this side of the gardens, turn right past the Maze and through a gateway in the wall ahead, go round the Garden Room and left into Tiltyard Gardens. Pass the Tiltyard Tea Rooms, go left through a gateway and continue straight ahead (passing WCs). The path leads out on to the lawns, gravel paths, flowerbeds and clipped yews behind the Palace. (To visit the Arboretum and Apprentice Gardens, an interesting and peaceful feature missed by most visitors, turn left and cross the lawn.) Turn right and walk along the back of the Palace, past the Tudor Tennis Courts to its centre point. Three paths radiate from here. Take the right-hand avenue through the three-centuries-old yew trees and pass through a side gate in the ornamental gateway into the Home Park.

Take the left-hand path along the avenue ahead and, when it joins an open road, continue along the road until it bears left at farm buildings. Leave the road here for a broad path straight ahead, pausing perhaps to sit by a small pond on the right which is covered in water-lilies in high summer. Bear left on a crossing path between golf greens, past the fenced Mediaeval Oak said to be more than 1,000 years old. When the path rejoins the road, cross to the banks of the Long Water and continue along the canal.

At the end of the canal there is a small pond with the larger Rick Pond further on to the right. (The path beside Rick Pond leads out to the Barge Walk along the River Thames.) Cross the road between the canal and the small pond and take a broad, grassy path half-left across the grass. Ignore a right fork towards a brick house and continue across the open park between road and fence towards a low tree-covered knoll. Continue along a railed track beyond the knoll, eventually joining the road to the left of a brick, 12-sided icehouse. Follow the road out of the park gate and turn right. *To return to Hampton Wick station*, go up the High Street past the White Hart. *To return to Kingston Bridge*, go round to the right. Across the bridge lies the old Surrey market town of Kingston, with its Coronation Stone where Saxon kings were crowned, the ancient Clattern Bridge and an abundance of pubs, restaurants and cafes.

EXTENSION: TO HAMPTON VILLAGE (1.5 MILES)

From the lake in the Woodland Gardens, turn right beside the waterfall, passing the summerhouse at the top of the lake, and follow the river to a gate. Go through the gate, turn right along an avenue to the fence of the Stockyard, then go through a gate on the left to the road outside the park. Turn right past Garrick's Villa, go up Church Street, then return down the High Street and in front of the church. Cross the road to Garrick's Lawn to see Shakespeare's Temple, Garrick's tribute to Shakespeare. Return by the gate into the park and retrace your steps to the lake to continue the walk.

CONNECTION WITH WALK 7

Cross Kingston Bridge and turn left along the riverside. Go through Canbury Gardens and follow the towpath to Teddington Lock. Turn right to connect with Walk 7 as it comes over Ham Riverside Lands.

> HAMPTON COURT PALACE GARDENS:
> This route is open free to the public throughout the year, except during the Hampton Court Flower Show in early July.
> Tel: 020 8781 9826.

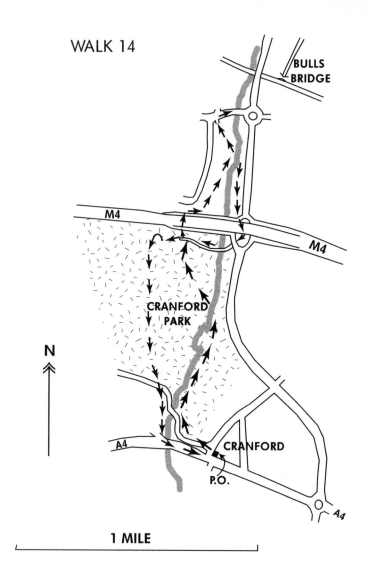

WALK 14

BULLS
BRIDGE

M4

M4

M4

CRANFORD
PARK

N

A4

CRANFORD

P.O.

A4

1 MILE

Cranford Park

Like many local parks, Cranford Park was once a small country estate and has retained its highly individual character along with some of its original features. Cranford Park has a ha-ha, a cobbled courtyard with high-walled stables and a classic bridge built by the Berkeleys, though the house itself has been demolished.

....

DISTANCE: 3.0 miles (circular). Connection to Walks 16 and 24 at Bulls Bridge on Extension.

EXTENSION: To canal towpaths and beyond.

TERRAIN: Mostly grass.

REFRESHMENTS: Pub on Bath Road near finish. Pub on North Hyde Road on Extension.

TRANSPORT: Buses 81, 222, H98 from Hounslow West station (Piccadilly Line) to junction of Bath Road and Cranford High Street. Go through the subway under Bath Road.

TRAVELCARD ZONE: 5. Zone 4 for buses.

STARTING POINT: Post office, Cranford High Street.

Go down Park Road, opposite the post office, and enter Avenue Park on the right. Turn left on a path and follow it into a strip of woodland, where the path bears right with the River Crane soon appearing on your left. Follow this path north, along the river, for almost the whole length of the Park. Just before the M4, follow it left round the last of a series of bends and into the wood. When you come to a footbridge, cross the river into Cranford Park. Walk half right across the open grass towards the fences of a children's playground and a car park, with the tower of St Dunstan's Church half hidden in trees beyond. Keeping to the right of the car park, go into the drive and turn left past the church into a cobbled courtyard with a circular hedge in the centre and a high stable wall beyond. The stables are all that is left above ground of Cranford House, which was demolished in 1945. For three centuries it was the home of the Berkeleys, who left in 1918.

Go through the left-hand arch of the stables and through the underpass under the M4. Turn right along the path, continuing below the motorway and then through woodland, following the Hillingdon Trail waymark posts until you reach an open grassy strip. Where the grassy strip widens, bear right to a footbridge. *The Extension to the canal towpath starts here.*

Cross the footbridge over the River Crane and follow the bridleway past the reputed site of the moated manor house of Cranford le Mote to a subway under the motorway intersection. Go under another subway on the right and continue on into Cranford Park. Cross the classic bridge and return to the courtyard.

Across the courtyard, a low brick building holds the entrance to the old cellars of Cranford House. Skirt the fence to the left of this building and follow a path beyond into the woods until you reach the ha-ha. Turn right and follow the ha-ha to a bridge. Cross the bridge and continue for a few yards, then fork left at a low waymark post and follow this path through the woods out into open parkland. Walk straight ahead over this wide expanse of grass; the exact line does not matter but keep roughly parallel with the hedge away to the right.

At the far end of the Park, as you approach Cranford Lane with its line of houses, aim for the fence at the edge of the woodland strip on your left with a signpost. But at whatever point you meet the road, turn left and cross over. Beyond the last house, turn into Berkeley Meads which soon has the Crane bordering it. Exit from the far end on to the Bath Road where you should turn right for the nearest bus stop and pub, or left to return to your starting point.

EXTENSION: TO CANAL TOWPATHS AND BEYOND

From the near side of the footbridge, continue along the river, in the direction of the Hillingdon Trail signpost. Leave the field by the far corner and go up to North Hyde Road (pub on left). Turn right, cross at traffic lights and follow the curving footpath up to the road bridge as it crosses the Grand Union Canal. A pedestrian and cycle zig-zag takes you down to the canal towpath just before the old, humpbacked Bulls Bridge which carries the towpath over the Paddington Arm. *From here you can go*: *west* to Hayes (0.7 mile, return from Hayes station) or for Walk 24, Stockley Park, West Drayton, Little Britain, Uxbridge and beyond; *east* to Three Bridges, Osterley, Boston Manor Park, Brentford and the Thames; or *north-east* up the Paddington Arm to Northolt, Greenford, Horsenden Hill, Alperton, Kensal Green and Paddington. *Or*, following the Hillingdon Trail signs, leave the Paddington Arm at Spikes Bridge (1.7 miles) and head north-west along the Yeading Brook and its meadows (Walk 16) and on through Ickenham and the Ruislip Woods to the Colne Valley.

Three Hills

This is an exhilarating walk with many opportunities for exploration. One Tree Hill gives only a taster of the impressive views and wide range of wildlife to be found on and around Horsenden Hill. Central, Metropolitan and Piccadilly Lines all have stations serving this area, so you can have a good tramp up and down the length of the ridge, then come back later to explore the meadows below Horsenden Hill and Harrow School's playing fields.

....

DISTANCE: 6.0 miles from Alperton (linear); 4.5 miles from Perivale. Connection with Walk 10 at Perivale.

EXTENSION: Over Harrow School playing fields and Northwick Park (2.5 miles).

TERRAIN: Mixed. Some of the paths on Horsenden Hill are rough and steep.

REFRESHMENTS: Clubhouse cafeteria and Ballot Box pub on Horsenden Hill. Pubs, cafes and restaurants in Harrow-on-the-Hill.

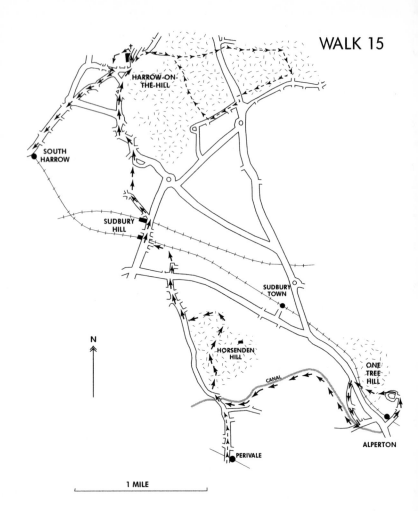

WALK 15

HARROW-ON-THE-HILL

SOUTH HARROW

SUDBURY HILL

SUDBURY TOWN

HORSENDEN HILL

ONE TREE HILL

CANAL

ALPERTON

PERIVALE

N

1 MILE

TRANSPORT: Piccadilly Line to Alperton station. Buses 79, 83, 297 (224, 245, 487 nearby). Central Line to Perivale.
TRAVELCARD ZONES: 4 (5 to return from South Harrow or Harrow-on-the-Hill stations).
STARTING POINT: Alperton station.
ALTERNATIVE STARTING POINT: Perivale station. Turn right out of the station up Horsenden Lane South to the canal bridge.

....

Turn left out of Alperton station, pass shops and turn left up St James Gardens. Turn right at the T-junction and, at the top, go straight across the grass to the highest point of One Tree Hill and pause to enjoy the view. Beyond the trig point, continue straight ahead downhill, pass a children's play area and turn left on a tarmac path under the railway.

Cross Bridgewater Road and go down Clifford Road opposite; this curves to meet Manor Farm Road at the far end. Cross Manor Farm Road and turn right over the canal bridge. Go left down steps to the canal towpath and left again under the bridge. Continue along the canal for just over 1 mile to the next bridge, with the slopes of Horsenden Hill gradually rising from the far bank. When you reach the bridge, leave the canal and turn right. *Walk 10 and the route from Perivale station up Horsenden Lane South join here.*

Cross the pedestrian bridge and continue a few yards along the road. Pass the entrance to Horsenden Farm and take the next opening to the right. At a noticeboard with a map, take the middle sandy path, the steepest one. The path climbs, passing belts of trees and open ground, and crossing other tracks. At the second crossing track, turn left and contour round to an open, flat area. At the far end, turn right, over a line of logs, and continue straight up to the summit. Some areas are fenced off to help control erosion, but any path going uphill will lead you to the trig point on the summit. Horsenden Hill is 84m (276ft) high and the views from various points of the summit meadow range from Canary Wharf to Harrow Church, our next objective.

From the trig point, face Harrow Church to the north and return towards the broad track you came up. On the track, turn to your right, passing a couple of seats on your right. Go downhill into the wood, bearing slightly left to keep away from a golf green. Continue downhill on a broad, earthen path through Horsenden Wood to a metalled crossing track.

For refreshments and WCs, turn right on this track and right again beside a small car park to the golf clubhouse beyond.

For Sudbury Town station, pass the small car park and take a diagonal path across the grass into trees and down an alleyway. Turn right down Ashness Gardens and cross over to Crossgates and up to the station. (If using this route in reverse, look for the alleyway between numbers 59 and 61.)

Continue on the earthen path through the middle of

the wood as far as the fenced areas allow, aiming for houses visible at the far corner of the wood. When you reach Whitton Drive and Rosewood Avenue, take the left-hand tarmac path through trees, signed to Horsenden Lane North. This emerges beside the Ballot Box pub, once a polling station used by canal folk on a site closer to the canal. (Across the road is the start of a path that crosses the lower fields to an elegant bridge over the canal. The path beyond leads to Greenford station (Central Line and Thames Trains) – opportunity for further explorations.)

Turn right along Horsenden Lane North, which continues as Melville Avenue, cross over Whitton Avenue and go up Rosehill Gardens opposite. At the top, turn left along the strip of green, continuing past Allen Court to Greenford Road. Turn right, crossing over at the lights, go past Sudbury Hill station (Piccadilly Line) and Sudbury Hill Harrow station (mainline), then turn left up South Vale. At the end, where it turns sharply left, keep right and go straight on up a clear, stony track. This climbs steadily up to Sudbury Hill. There is a narrow, earthen footpath through the trees alongside. Continue up the road ahead. You will pass many fine properties, with gardens sloping steeply down from the ridge you are climbing. Cross Roxeth Hill and continue ahead along London Road and through the town of Harrow-on-the-Hill until the left-hand pavement divides at Church Hill. Harrow-on-the-Hill has many fine buildings, mostly connected with the school. *The Extension across the school playing fields and Northwick Park begins at the foot of Church Hill.*

Go up Church Hill, where you can catch glimpses over London from between the buildings on the right. Pass the gates of the Old Schools to reach the lychgate opposite a balustrade overlooking the Speech Room and War Memorial building. Enter the churchyard, bearing left, and pass the church door – the church is usually open during the daytime, except on Fridays. Beyond the church is the terrace, with a long view to the south-west and an orientation plaque. Behind the benches, there is a stone panel with lines written by Byron, who would sit and gaze at this view.

The tarmac path to the right leads to a road where a footpath sign points to Harrow-on-the-Hill Met. station. To complete the exploration of Harrow, continue straight ahead, down the steps between the plaque and the churchyard to a field known as High Capers. Take the left-hand path down the field, aiming to the left of a hedge at the bottom of the field, and join a tarmac path. Follow this to the left around several corners until you reach West Street. Turn left up to the Castle pub, then right down Crown Street and right into Middle Road, past many interesting buildings, then straight down Northolt Road, the modern main road, *to South Harrow Piccadilly Line station.*

EXTENSION: OVER HARROW SCHOOL PLAYING FIELDS AND NORTHWICK PARK (2.5 MILES)

From the foot of Church Hill, continue along Peterborough Road and, just beyond the brow, go down Football Lane on the right. Where the lane turns right, keep straight ahead downhill on a path to the playing fields. At the footpath signpost, the arm for Watford Road and Pebworth Road should point your way. You need to head approximately straight ahead (slightly left if anything) across the sports pitches towards a wide gap in the distant hedge. Before you reach the gap, bear to the left of a triangular patch of rough grass. Continue, with the pitches on your left, until you can follow a hedge on the right to the corner of the field where there is a stile out to the Watford Road.

Cross to the Ducker footpath opposite. Follow it through a patch of woodland then, with Northwick Park Hospital on your left, out into Northwick Park. Continue ahead by any of the paths along the left edge of the park to the playing fields, then turn right on a tarmac path through a small car park (WCs in the sports pavilion on the left). Continue beside the drive, turning right just before the exit. *For South Kenton station turn left outside.* Walk along the southern edge of the park. There is a splendid view ahead of the slopes of the hill. At the end of the field, follow a fenced path to the Watford Road, cross over and plod up Pebworth Road. Between numbers 56 and 58, turn right along an alleyway and go over the stile, back into the open fields. Keeping the spires of Harrow ahead and slightly to your left, go up to the far left-hand corner. Cross a metal bar stile and go through a wooden kissing gate. Beyond another gate, follow the right-hand line of young trees down to more metal bars and back to the sports pitches. Continue straight ahead between two of them and to the right of a third, back to the signpost at the foot of Football Lane. Return up the lane ahead, turn left at Peterborough Road and cross over at a pedestrian crossing. Climb the steps to Church Hill by the Old Schools to continue the walk.

Yeading Brook Meadows

This walk follows the Yeading Brook through open fields, ancient woodland, farmland, and meadows with over 100 different species of wild flower. The walk follows the brook for several miles along its banks, with no need to set foot on a road except to cross over. Further down its course, the brook becomes the River Crane, which features in other walks as it runs through Cranford Park and Crane River Park.

....

DISTANCE: 3.7 or 6.0 miles (linear). Connections with Walk 14 at Bulls Bridge and Walk 24 at Hayes, both on the Extension.

EXTENSION: To Hayes (2.0 miles).

TERRAIN: Level. Rough grass, several stiles.

REFRESHMENTS: Pubs on Kingshill Avenue, Yeading Lane and Uxbridge Road.

TRANSPORT: Central Line. Bus E7.

TRAVELCARD ZONE: 5. Zone 4 for buses.

STARTING POINT: Ruislip Gardens station

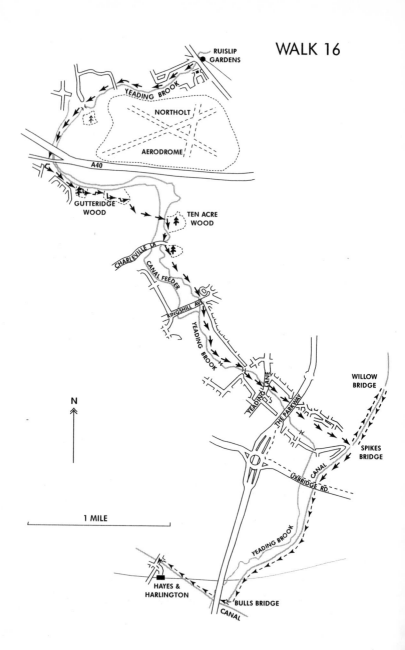

WALK 16

RUISLIP GARDENS

YEADING BROOK

NORTHOLT

AERODROME

GUTTERIDGE WOOD

TEN ACRE WOOD

CHARLEVILLE LA

CANAL FEEDER

KINGSHILL AVE

YEADING BROOK

N

1 MILE

WILLOW BRIDGE

YEADING LANE

THE PARKWAY

SPIKES BRIDGE

A40

UXBRIDGE RD.

CANAL

YEADING BROOK

HAYES & HARLINGTON

BULLS BRIDGE

CANAL

Turn right out of the station, cross the road and take the path to the right of the Yeading Brook. Follow the path, keeping beside the brook for about a mile. Drop down to cross a ditch in a small copse. Beyond, the path leaves the brook briefly, and crosses the grass ahead. The crossing path leads to an information panel beside a footbridge. This footbridge leads to Ickenham Marsh Nature Reserve, which is open to the public. Continue along the brook again.

Follow the Hillingdon Trail signs and go underneath both sections of Western Avenue A40. Turn right beyond the second section, then left and left again, round the edge of a line of houses and into an open space. Keep on the tarmac path across the field and at the HT signpost, turn left into a path between a hedge and back gardens and continue along this for 100 yards. Continue on past an HT waymark and, at the next wide gap in the hedge, turn into a field and cross the field towards a signpost at the far end. Go through the metal kissing gates into Gutteridge Wood.

Leave the track marked with white arrows to take the first right-hand fork. When this path meets a crossing path in the open, turn left on it, back into the wood. When you reach the brook, turn right. Continue on this track through the wood, on duckboards over damp areas, turning left at an HT signpost in the middle of the wood and left again at one on the edge of the wood. Continue on this path to the far end of the wood. You will reach a signpost, footbridge and stile leading out into fields. Follow the waymarks to the right.

At the next signpost, ignore the stile which leads to the Seven Stiles Way and turn left on a winding path through bushes. Go over a stile into a fenced path between fields. Cross a footbridge into North Meadow and continue along the left edge of the meadow, past the information panel and over a footbridge into Ten Acre Wood. Follow the HT route to the right. At the next signpost, where the HT leaves the wood for the fields on the right, continue ahead on a path which stays in the wood a little longer before it comes out into the open at some steps. Turn right at the top of the steps and rejoin the HT as it crosses a bridge over the brook. Follow a gravel track out on to Charville Lane beside Westways Farm. (This lane, an old route which is marked on some very early maps, continues beyond the farm as Sharvel Lane and passes the old moated site of Downe Barns Farm.)

Cross over the Golden Bridge opposite Westways Farm and turn left on a gravel track. Just before a gate, turn right into woods past a West London Waterways waymark, and follow the path out into the open meadow. Follow the path on the left-hand side of the meadow, or keep beside the brook.

After about half a mile you reach Kingshill Avenue (3.7 miles) where bus 90 goes to Northolt station (Central Line) in one direction, and Hayes and Harlington, Hatton Cross or Feltham in the other. The E9 bus to

Ealing Broadway (Mondays to Saturdays only) comes up Ayles Road, a little further to the left.

To continue, cross the road to the meadow opposite. Keep along the right-hand edge of the short grass until the brook emerges from its windings through scrub. (Paths do cross this wild, flower-rich fringe but can be difficult to access at certain times of year.) Ignore the first footbridge, cross the second and continue, at an HT signpost, along the other side of the brook. Cross Yeading Lane (pub on right), turn left to cross the brook and continue along the left bank. Follow the brook through a gap in a hedge into the next field, then cross diagonally towards a fence and drop down through the subway under the Hayes Bypass.

Beyond the subway, continue along the left-hand side of the playing fields, past an HT waymark post, on a rough path through bushes. Ignore the HT signpost pointing to the left (this leads past a marina to a pleasant picnic spot near Willow Bridge, which crosses the canal half a mile further north). Continue until you reach houses, where you should turn left on to a tarmac path leading to the canal. Cross Spikes Bridge, turn down to the left and under the bridge and follow the canal towpath south for 0.3 mile to Uxbridge Road. Buses 207, 607 go to Ealing Broadway station.

EXTENSION: TO HAYES (2.0 MILES)

Continue on the canal towpath underneath Uxbridge Road for over a mile to Bulls Bridge, an old humpback bridge which carries the Grand Union Canal towpath over the Paddington Arm. Turn right to station Road, Hayes, where you can catch buses, a train from Hayes and Harlington station, or continue under the road to connect with Walk 24.

Ickenham to Uxbridge via Swakeleys and Denham

The Piccadilly Line runs to the very furthest western fringe of London. This walk starts in the village heart of suburban Ickenham. It takes in the magnificent Jacobean Swakeleys and its parkland and drops down into the Colne Valley, a rural landscape of branching water channels and willow-fringed scenery. The Extension crosses the Colne into Buckinghamshire on a winding woodland walk to Denham, one of the prettiest villages in the countryside around London.

....

DISTANCE: 4.0 miles (linear).

EXTENSION: Denham Country Park and village (3.0 miles).

TERRAIN: Tarmac, earthen paths and bridleways.

REFRESHMENTS: Pubs in Ickenham, on Harefield Road and in Uxbridge. Cafes and snack bars in Uxbridge. On Extension: lock-keeper's cottage at Denham Lock, pubs

WALK 17

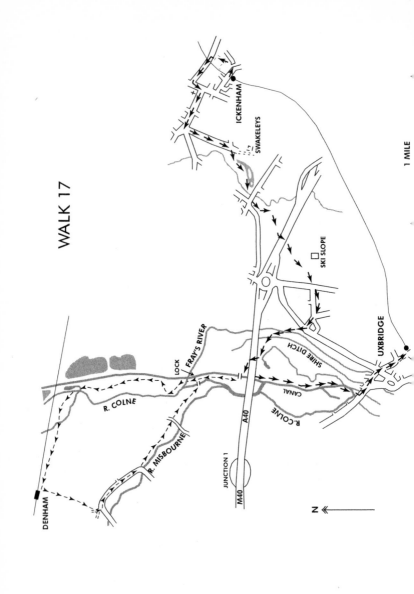

DENHAM

R. COLNE

R. MISBOURNE

LOCK

FRAY'S RIVER

R. COLNE

SHIRE DITCH

CANAL

R.COLNE

JUNCTION 1

M40

A40

SKI SLOPE

UXBRIDGE

SWAKELEYS

ICKENHAM

N

1 MILE

in Denham village, tea bar in Denham Country Park
Visitors Centre.
TRANSPORT: Piccadilly and Metropolitan Lines. Bus U1
to Ickenham village, U10 to Ickenham station.
TRAVELCARD ZONE: 6. Zone 4 for buses.
STARTING POINT: Ickenham station.

....

From the station, cross the road, turn right and continue
for about 70 yards. Go down steps, turn right, then turn
left down Lawrence Drive. Look for an alleyway next to
number 72 and follow this into a field. Cross the field,
passing playground equipment, to the far corner, and
exit into Austin's Lane. Turn left along this quiet
country lane, crossing over the railway and passing an
old barn, out to Ickenham High Road. Turn left past the
Tudor farmhouse, old cottages, pub, tiny pond and
Victorian village pump. St Giles's Church is opposite.
This was the heart of the original village of Ickenham,
which survived well into the 20th century. Cross the
pedestrian crossing to Swakeleys Road and walk along
the parade of shops. Beyond the shops, turn left down
The Avenue. Houses on the right soon give way to a
little copse and then the open space of Swakeleys.

Keep straight ahead to a high gate, labelled SHBC,
where you should turn right on a path alongside the
fence. Just before this path joins others at a small bridge
at the end of a lake, a gateway on the left leads to a view
of Swakeleys. The house was built between 1629 and

1638 by Sir Edmund Wright, a City alderman, later Lord Mayor, and has had several owners. Pepys records a visit here in 1666. It is now company offices and is open to the public three times a year. The dates can be obtained from Hillingdon local libraries.

Turn back to the gateway, cross the bridge and follow the surfaced path beside the lake (or cross the grass to the River Pinn beyond and turn left on the grassy path beside it). Both paths lead to Swakeleys Drive. Turn right to cross the river, then cross the road to a tarmac cycle/pedestrian track which soon turns sharp left into woods. Stay on the tarmac path when it forks right and continue to the high bridleway bridge over the busy Western Avenue A40.

On the far side of the bridge, go through a metal zig-zag on to a footpath beside a bridleway and follow the path through woodland. Where the main path bends right, continue on an earthen path for a few yards out into open playing fields. The field on the left has a ski slope on the far side. Follow the hedge on the right-hand side of this field, on a path which starts to the left of the hedge. A view of a square, brick water tower lies ahead. This path then crosses between sports fields and follows a hedge on the left-hand side of the field to a gate leading out to Park Road.

Cross over Park Road to North Common Road opposite and walk down North Common Road, or along the edge of Uxbridge Common. There is a view over open country ahead. At the far corner, beyond the pond, turn right down Gravel Hill and then left at the end. After 30 yards, just before the Arbrook Arms pub, turn right down a farm drive (a public footpath). Continue alongside the Fray's River, then cross the river on a small concrete footbridge with handrail, and turn right. The path along the river is narrow and care must be taken in wet weather, but it soon turns away and continues underneath a disused railway line. It runs over marshy ground (as a board walk) beside the Shire Ditch (the boundary between Middlesex and Buckinghamshire) before crossing the Ditch.

The path eventually passes underneath the A40. On the far side, ignore the track climbing up to the road, and take the footpath which starts beside it. This winds its way, beneath the road embankment but with a lovely view of the countryside, to the Grand Union Canal where the towpath crosses a humpback bridge. *The Extension to Denham Country Park and village, or a brief diversion for refreshments at Denham Lock, starts here.*

To finish the walk, do not cross the bridge but turn left on the towpath to go back under the noisy A40, then follow the canal for a peaceful 0.7 mile to Uxbridge. The towpath crosses the canal at Uxbridge Lock. At the next road bridge, climb steps up to the pavement in front of the Swan and Bottle pub, and turn left on the Oxford Road. Cross the canal and a side turning, then leave the main road to continue over Fray's River and up the High Street. The Underground station is at the far end of the pedestrianised stretch of the High Street, and the bus station is behind it.

EXTENSION: DENHAM COUNTRY PARK AND VILLAGE (3.0 MILES)

Cross the humpback bridge and follow the towpath to Denham Lock. The garden of the lock cottage, with a dovecote and a view of the River Colne, provides refreshments. Ignore the footpath signs just below the lock and continue a few yards beyond the lock to some steps. Go down the steps, cross a bridge over Fray's River and continue to a board walk beside the River Colne. When this path reaches a solid wooden bridge, do not cross it but turn right and continue until you reach a wooden signpost pointing to Denham Quarry, from where you can see the high bridge crossing the canal.

Do not turn up to the canal, but continue straight ahead for about a mile, through woodland and along the edge of fields. Continue past an elegant white-painted footbridge and cross the Colne on a long, wooden footbridge and then cross another of its channels. The viaduct ahead carries the main line from Marylebone high over the Colne valley. As the path approaches one of the arches over the river, it bends left to keep underneath the embankment, with a golf course on the left. When the path turns left to meet a tarmac path, the right-hand branch leads to Denham station (outside the Travelcard zone). The parallel bridle and footpaths lead to Denham village, so turn left. When the brick wall of Denham Place appears beside you, follow it to the village along The Pyghtle.

The village green has benches and there are three pubs within view. To the right of the green, a narrow bridge crosses the River Misbourne. *The road beyond continues rightwards to a main road where buses run to Uxbridge, but not all routes may accept your Travelcard.* Most of old Denham lies the other direction from the green, so walk up past the three pubs and the church and continue along the road. Shortly after passing Court Farm, the road bends. Opposite Mill House and Wellers Mead, either side of the mill stream, a public footpath sign points left. Follow this sign, going through two kissing gates on to a golf course. Keep to the left of a fence, then go across a short stretch of open grass, following the waymarks, and continue to the right of the next line of fence. The path goes through another kissing gate and continues ahead, but you may want to visit the Colne Valley Park Visitors Centre in the building on your right (WCs, snack bar, exhibition and information office). Cross the field diagonally to return to the sandy path and you may find some interesting creatures!

Follow the path out through a kissing gate, cross a drive and go through another gate. Continue on the sandy path ahead, signposted South Bucks Way, under pylon lines along Misbourne Meadow. Go through another gate, cross a bridge and return to the canal towpath, where you should turn right to return to the humpback bridge. Follow the instructions at end of main walk to finish at Uxbridge.

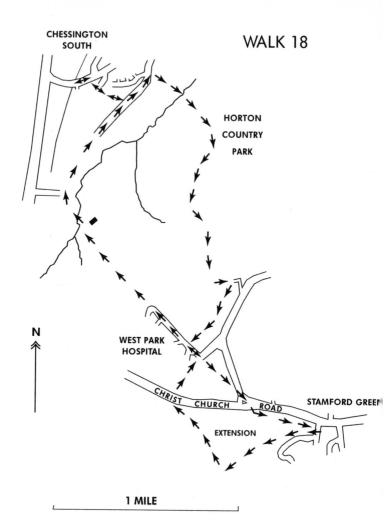

WALK 18

CHESSINGTON
SOUTH

HORTON

COUNTRY

PARK

N

WEST PARK
HOSPITAL

CHRIST   CHURCH   ROAD

STAMFORD GREEN

EXTENSION

1 MILE

Horton Country Park and Epsom Common

This walk takes you straight into the countryside, only half an hour's journey by train from Waterloo. From the ridge above the Bonesgate Stream there are fine views over the wooded expanse of Epsom and Ashtead Commons to the North Downs beyond.

....

DISTANCE: 4.0 miles (circular).

EXTENSION: Epsom Common (2.0 miles).

TERRAIN: Rough grass.

REFRESHMENTS: Public bar and cafe in Golf Centre opposite station. Farm Centre cafe. Pub on Stamford Green on Extension.

TRANSPORT: South West Trains. Bus 71. 465 and 568 (Mon–Sat) nearby.

TRAVELCARD ZONE: 6. Zone 4 for buses.

STARTING POINT: Chessington South station.

....

From the station, cross over the road and turn left. After 50 yards, go up the fenced path between houses at a footpath signpost. You soon come out on the edge of a golf green with outstanding views south over the woods of Epsom Common to the North Downs.

Turn left by the waymarks along the edge of the green, curving round rightwards to a stile leading to Green Lane. Cross over Green Lane, turn left and continue until you reach a stile on the right, opposite a small blocks of flats. Follow the narrow, hedged path over two more stiles, over a footbridge over the Bonesgate Stream and along the edge of two fields. Continue around the far side of the second field until you reach a stile halfway along. The path beyond leads to a junction of tracks.

Many of the footpaths through the Country Park follow the route of the Horton Light Railway. This was constructed at the start of the 20th century to carry building materials for the new Long Grove Hospital, and later to carry supplies to other hospitals on the Horton estate. The railway closed in 1950.

The CheSsington Countryside Walk goes straight ahead, but leave it to turn right along a track through trees. At the end of the meadow on the left, follow its fence round leftwards and continue to a T-junction, where you should turn right on to the main track. Keep on this track as it bears left past an equestrian centre to a small complex of buildings. There are WCs on the right, and the Country Park office, where you can look at displays and pick up walks leaflets and other useful material, is on the left.

To visit the Farm Centre (0.4 mile), which has a range of livestock (including rare or unusual breeds), a shop and a teashop, turn left through the buildings and through a gate with the sign 'Horton Park Farm'. Follow the enclosed path between open fields. The path turns right alongside the farm to a car park. The entrance to the farm, shop and teashop is across the car park. There is a charge for entry to the farm itself.

From the far side of the WCs building, follow the broad track on the right, which bends left through a picnic area. Just before it meets a road, follow waymark signs through a gate on the right. Keep on this track round a curve and continue ahead. Turn, at waymarks, through an opening in the fence on the left on to an earthern path which takes you into the wood and across a drive. This path ends at a crossing track and the grounds of West Park Hospital lie beyond a high fence. Underneath an overhead pipe on the left are wooden barriers. *The Extension to Epsom Common turns off in this direction.*

To complete the circuit to Chessington station, turn right and follow this rather narrow fenced path for 0.5 mile past hospital buildings and grounds until a stile leads out into open farmland. Follow the path ahead through fields, across the concrete farm drive, over another stile and half right across a field to a stile by a ditch. On the road, turn left past the cottages to a sharp left bend, where you should turn right at a footpath signpost on to a track signposted to Chessington, the start of Green Lane. The track, which further on becomes a surfaced road, leads back to the stile on to the golf green. Retrace your steps back to Chessington station.

EXTENSION: EPSOM COMMON (2.0 MILES)

At the crossing track, turn left through the wooden barriers under the overhead pipe out to a road. Pass the gates of West Park Hospital and cross over to the bridleway opposite (not the one on the right). At Horton Lane, turn right and take the right fork to Christchurch Road. Cross over and take the footpath opposite, bearing left and left again to remain in the wood, roughly parallel with the road. Pass the church in the trees, then take the next path on the left, crossing the church driveway. Continue through trees to Stamford Green. The Cricketers pub and a small pond with benches are across the green.

From the pond, re-cross the green, parallel with the church side, to a midpoint where a path leads into the trees half left, and keep left at a fork. Cross over the church drive and continue ahead for 0.5 mile, ignoring the first crossing track. The track widens. At the top of a rise, where tracks cross, there is a bench and Thames Down Link waymark. Turn right here, ignore a left fork and keep straight on for 0.4 mile.

As the track approaches the road, follow the signs for Thames Down Link and Chessington Countryside Walk. (The track you are leaving leads to the Stew Pond and Great Pond above it, and also, following the Chessington Countryside Walk waymarks in that direction, back to Chessington station by another, longer route over Winey Hill, above the World of Adventures.) Cross the road to the bridleway opposite, which leads back to West Park Hospital where you should turn left on the footpath to complete the walk, as in the main route directions.

HORTON PARK FARM CENTRE:
Open daily. Summer 10a.m.–6p.m.,
Winter 10a.m.–5p.m.
Closed Christmas Day and Boxing Day.
Teashop closes half an hour before farm.

WALK 19

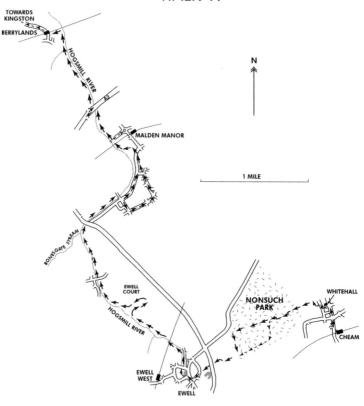

Nonsuch Park and the River Hogsmill

This is a walk with much historical interest. It is worth paying a visit, at the start of the walk, to Whitehall in Cheam so that as you cross the now empty expanse of Nonsuch Park you can visualise the grandeur of the Tudor palace which it once surrounded. Ewell Village – Church Street, High Street and the ponds formed by the Hogsmill springs – is picturesque. As the route heads downstream, houses and streets give way to willows and riverside meadows. The main route leaves the river before it enters the built-up area beyond Berrylands. The Extension continues on to Kingston's Saxon Coronation Stone and the 12th-century Clattern Bridge.

....

DISTANCE: 6.0 miles to Malden Manor station (linear), 7.3 miles to Berrylands station. This walk passes several bus routes and can be divided into shorter sections.
EXTENSION: To Kingston (1.7 miles).
TERRAIN: Level, mostly grass paths.

REFRESHMENTS: Pubs in Cheam, Ewell, Malden Manor and Berrylands. Cafes in Nonsuch Park and at Bourne Hall.

TRANSPORT: South Central Connex Trains. Buses 151, 213, 408 (Mon–Sat), 726.

TRAVELCARD ZONE: 6

STARTING POINT: Cheam station for trains. The Broadway, Cheam for buses.

....

From the down platform go through the subway under the lines to the further exit, then follow the road facing it to station Way, opposite the Railway pub, and turn right. Cross the road junction at the traffic lights and continue up The Broadway, on the left-hand pavement past shops and the 'Old Cottage'. A hundred yards further on is Whitehall, a beautiful, white weatherboarded 16th-century house, now a local museum. To the right of the house there is a map and brief details of other interesting buildings in Cheam.

Go down the road to the left of Whitehall passing more weatherboarded houses, old and new. Turn right into Cheam Park Way and left into Cheam Park past a brick hut to join a tarmac path. Turn right on the path, follow its curves to a crossing path at the yard gates of the park nursery and turn left along the wall. When the tarmac ends, continue across the grass under trees to the edge of a strip of woodland, and take an earthen path into the woodland near its right-hand edge. The path soon runs along the edge of some fields. Enter the second field and go round the high brick wall. Just round the corner, a gate in the fence leads to the Aviary. Continue along the fence past the gate to a driveway and go through the arched brick gateway into the gardens of Nonsuch Mansion (WCs on the right inside the gateway). Walk past the garden front and right round to the grand front entrance. (The cafe is just beyond the porch.) The mansion house was built in 1804, in Georgian Gothic style, by Wyatville, incorporating a former farmhouse as its kitchen wing. It is not open to the public.

Take the path on the left past the gardens out into the open expanse of Nonsuch Park. (If you prefer to keep to the tarmac path, follow it as it bends leftwards to the avenue along the southern edge of the park and turn right.) To cross the open park, continue on a faint path through the grass. Keep to the left of a small copse, on the middle path. This path eventually runs beside a ditch lined with trees. Follow this to a tarmac path coming from a car park and turn left. You soon pass three low, granite pillars which record the site of Nonsuch Palace and the village of Cuddington demolished to make way for it; the first one has a brass plaque inset showing the ground plan of the palace only revealed in excavations in 1959–60. Nonsuch Palace, a richly decorated hunting lodge, was built by Henry VIII to celebrate the birth of his son. The pillars mark the sites of the outer and inner gatehouses and the centre bay of the south front. Less than 150 years after it was built, this small but magnificent building was demolished. Charles II's mistress Barbara Villiers sold it off as building stone and the site was forgotten. It took detective work as well as archaeology to discover the site in 1959.

Continue down the path where it meets the southern avenue at a lodge. *The tarmac path rejoins here.* Turn right past a numbered bollard and continue on an earthen path through trees, with a field to the right. Continue to follow the bollards, which mark the Nonsuch Trail, and turn right at number 5 to the bastioned corner of the platform wall on which the banqueting house of the palace once stood. (It served as a grandstand to watch the hunt.) Go past bollard 6 to the end of the field and turn left, following a hedge to a fence and steps in the right-hand corner. (Beyond the hedge, the steep slopes, now a natural adventure playground, were dug out as claypits for the Nonsuch Potteries.) Go down to the main road. Cross over and, on the service road beyond, go down the steps to Vicarage Lane, a muddy track which imporoves as it nears the church.

You emerge in Ewell Village between a disused church and Ewell Castle, an early 19th-century Gothic building that is now a school. Continue down Church Street, passing Well House, built in 1700, and down to the tiny Watch House on the corner of the High Street. Ewell also has several jettied timber-framed houses and shops. Turn right to the pedestrian lights (WCs 50 yards further on), cross to the opposite pavement (buses 293, 406, K10) and enter Bourne Hall Park through the beautiful white gateway. The pond outside the gateway is one of the sources of the Hogsmill River. Inside the gate, follow the path beside the lake. The original Bourne Hall has been demolished. The modern, circular building above the lawn houses a public library, a local history display, a small cafe and WCs (closed Wednesdays and Sundays.) Beyond the lake and its arch flanked by classical statues, leave the park through a gate leading on to Chessington Road beside the Horse Pond. (Ewell West station is a short distance away on the left, but is outside the Travelcard area.) Cross the road and turn right over another pond then walk down beside it and continue along the tarmac path. At a crossing drive, go round the front of the restored Upper Mill, crossing over the Hogsmill, then turn right down a path beside the river. (A mill on this site was recorded in the Domesday Book.) Continue along this path on the left bank of the river, through a strip of woodland crossing minor channels. The path goes underneath the railway on a long boardwalk above the river. Turn right on the track beyond, then immediately left to continue along on the right bank on a grassy path. A little further on, another stream joins the Hogsmill.

After 0.5 mile, you reach another path crossing the river on five stepping stones. Fork right here, keeping to the right of an area of rough grass and scrub, and pass the end of a street to meet a fenced crossing track. This path leads to Ewell Court Lake, well worth a few minutes' diversion. Turn right and follow the fence right round the head of the lake to the far side, where there are gardens, benches and picnic tables in front of Ewell Court (WCs in the building). Continue along the right-hand side of the stream and bend rightwards with the tarmac path as another one joins it from the wooded area on the far side. Go out through a gate towards a bridge, then continue again along the right-hand bank of the river, again on grass. (Alternative paths along the open grass higher up might be better in very wet conditions.) Cross over a tarmac path to continue by the river to Ruxley Lane. (Buses 479, K9.) Cross over Ruxley Lane and continue, past a small weir and line of willows. After 0.5 mile, just below an iron-railed footbridge, the Bonesgate Stream joins the Hogsmill, flowing past the open fields of Tolworth Court Farm. The path soon reaches Kingston Road (Buses 406, 479. Tolworth station half a mile to the left).

Cross Kingston Road at the traffic lights to the left-hand pavement of Worcester Park Road, then turn back a few yards, crossing over the river to a kissing gate which leads to the lower stretch of the Hogsmill Walk. This narrow, stony track continues for 0.4 mile between river and sports fields until it ends at a drive, where you must turn back to the road. Cross over to the Hogsmill pub. The next stretch of the river, where it runs through The Hollows, is inaccessible. The riverside path begins again 0.5 mile down Old Malden Lane, half of it without any pavement. For a slightly longer route back to the river, on quieter roads, walk up Cromwell Road and turn left into Grafton Road. In front of St Mary's Church, turn left and go through bollards on a gravel track which continues as Royal Avenue. At the end above Barrow Hill, continue straight ahead on a footpath through woodland to rejoin the lower road. Cross to the pavement, turn right for 50 yards then turn down a driveway signed to the Manor House. This leads to the lychgate of St John the Baptist's Church, Old Malden, which has some medieval stonework, and to the 18th-century brick Manor House. Beyond the lychgate, pass Manor Farm Cottage and follow the path (signposted Hogsmill Walk) down the hill. The path rejoins the river at a footbridge and continues under the railway viaduct to a crossing path and another footbridge.

For Malden Manor station (6.0 miles), turn right here up the path, which continues as a road, to a small roundabout. Go right past The Manor pub to reach the station.

To continue to Berrylands, continue along the right bank. Go out through a side gate on to the A3. Turn left over the river and cross under the road using the subway (at a line of shops). Turn back on the far side to a tall gate beside a bus stop (bus 265) and continue down the left-hand bank of the river. Near houses, the path takes you across a small stream then continues beside the river again towards the railway embankment ahead. As you approach the embankment, you see the Hogsmill disappearing under it into a sewage works beyond. The path turns to follow the embankment to Berrylands station. For buses, turn left up Chiltern Drive and cross the road at the top for the K2 bus to Surbiton and Kingston.

EXTENSION: TO KINGSTON (1.7 MILES)

Go under the railway beside Berrylands station into Lower Marsh Lane, following Hogsmill Walk signs. Turn right at Villiers Road, cross over the river, then go left down a footpath and continue following the signposts down a network of paths and streets. From Clattern Bridge at the end you can see the Hogsmill enter the Thames. You have followed it all the way from source to mouth.

> WHITEHALL:
> Open April–Sep Tues–Fri 2p.m.–5.30p.m.;
> Sat 10a.m.–5.30p.m.; Sun and bank holidays
> 2p.m.–5.30p.m.;
> Oct–March Wed–Thurs 2p.m.–5.30p.m.; Sat
> 10a.m.–5.30p.m.; Sun 2p.m.–5.30p.m.
> Closed Christmas Eve to January 2nd, and Good
> Friday.

Barn Hill, Fryent Country Park and Welsh Harp

This is a fine, hilly walk with long views and plenty to see nearby. Barn Hill, the ancient meadows and hedges of Fryent Country Park and the wide waters, teeming with bird life, of the Welsh Harp seem worlds away from London's streets. Kingsbury also has some surprises – the Trobridge houses on Slough Lane and Bucks Lane, and the contrast of its old and new parish churches.

....

DISTANCE: 5.0 miles (circular). 4.0 miles finishing at Blackbird Hill.

EXTENSION: A loop round the Trobridge houses area of Kingsbury (1.0 mile).

TERRAIN: Hilly, rough paths.

REFRESHMENTS: Pubs and cafes in Wembley and Blackbird Hill and at the top of Slough Lane on the Extension.

TRANSPORT: Jubilee and Metropolitan Lines. Buses 83, 182, 223 (Mon–Sat), 297, PR2 (245 nearby).

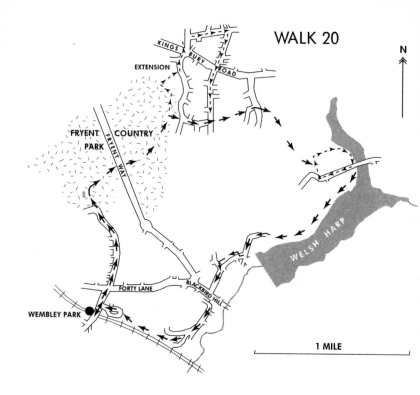

WALK 20

N

EXTENSION

KINGS BURY ROAD

FRYENT COUNTRY PARK

FRYENT WAY

WELSH HARP

FORTY LANE

BLACKBIRD HILL

WEMBLEY PARK

1 MILE

TRAVELCARD ZONE: 4

STARTING POINT: Wembley Park station.

....

Turn left up Bridge Road and cross Forty Lane.
Continue up the road ahead, Barn Hill, to reach open
ground at the top. Go between low posts beside a
noticeboard and bear left, climbing up a broad grassy
clearing between trees to the trig point at the top above
a pond. There are long views south across London, over
the turrets of Wembley Stadium. Go to the right of the
pond. Ignore a faint path and a few yards further on,
turn right on a crossing path into the trees. This
continues down an avenue of Lombardy poplars and
drops down to an open meadow, where a footpath
signpost indicates you are crossing an old track called
Eldestrete, also known as Hell Lane and formerly a
parish boundary between Harrow and Kingsbury.
Continue towards the road, Fryent Way, forking right
on a path leading to some rough steps. Cross the road to
a path to the right of a hedge, pass a red gas indicator
and cross a couple of ditches. The path continues along
the left side of a hedge, keeping on a ridge with fields
and hedges spreading below and a panorama of the
North London hills beyond.

Fryent Country Park is of particular interest for the
wild flowers of its meadows and ancient hedges. These
are not enclosure plantings; the shrubs they contain,
such as hazel, woodland hawthorn and wild service tree,

show that they are remnants of the woodland out of which the fields were cut perhaps 700 years ago. After 150 yards, fork left on a path dropping to a solitary oak tree. Beyond this, fork right towards a wide gap in the next hedge, and fork right again in the next field. Beyond the next hedge, the path runs beside the fence of a paddock, with views back to Barn Hill and Harrow-on-the-Hill beyond.

At the fence corner, *the Extension loop to pub and Trobridge houses starts at a footpath signpost.* If not following this, turn right along the other side of the paddock, past stables to some noticeboards, one of which gives details of the history of this area and its current management. Go out through barriers to Slough Lane where it turns a right angle, cross and go up the road straight ahead to a small shopping parade at Church Lane. *The Extension rejoins here.* Cross and go through gates into a small recreation ground (WCs). Cross the grass, or go round the left edge if the pitches are in use, to join a road at the far left corner, Elthorne Way, and follow this to a road with a children's playground opposite and an open field beyond. Cross the field half right to a gap between the end of a line of garden fences and a hedge. Turn right beyond the gap and follow the hedge along the edge of two sports pitches. At the end of the second one, bear slightly left uphill away from the line of houses on a broad grassy path between shrubs and small trees, climbing up to a low ridge, and turn left along the edge of another sports pitch.

At a line of trees at the end of this pitch you have a choice. The most direct route to the Brent Reservoir is to cross to the right-hand corner of the pitch and follow a path leftwards which drops down to Cool Oak Lane. Follow the lane for 0.3 mile to the bridge over the upper arm of the Brent Reservoir. To avoid this stretch of road, turn left at the fence at the end of the pitch, then follow the fence round to the right on a path which winds through a wild area. Continue right on a joining path until you come out at the shore of the upper arm of the reservoir. Turn right and follow the shore to the bridge where the road route rejoins.

Do not cross the bridge, but cross the road to a path opposite, past noticeboards.

The River Brent was dammed in 1835 to increase water supplies for the Grand Union Canal and its locks. (The borough boundary shown on maps still wriggling its way back and forth along much of the reservoir length preserves the original course of the river.) A popular alehouse, the Old Welsh Harp, gave its name to the reservoir which was a popular place of resort for 50 years. Today sailing and birdwatching – there are some 145 species of bird – are the most popular activities.

The path follows the north bank of the reservoir for nearly a mile, for the most part on a bank above the marshy shoreline – a pleasant walk with only the distant roar of the North Circular to intrude on the peaceful scene. Near the end, with the spire of Kingsbury Church ahead, the path joins tarmac and comes out in Birchen

Grove. Walk down the road as far as a block of red brick, red-tiled flats, then turn right up a short stretch of road as far as a gate. To the right of the gate, take a path into a churchyard, first keeping along the edge, then passing the old church of St Andrew to reach the new church. The old church, no longer in use and now cared for by Wembley History Society, dates probably from the early 13th century, though some Roman tiles and Saxon stones are incorporated in its walls. After many attempts at restoration it was finally closed. The new St Andrew's, a fine neo-Gothic church, was built near Oxford Circus in 1847, and became famous as a centre of Anglo-Catholicism. When this church was declared redundant it was transported to Kingsbury, complete with its fine interior furnishings.

Drop down to the road and go immediately left then right down Old Church Lane to Blackbird Hill. *To finish here* (4.0 miles), buses 182 and 297 return to Wembley Park station (also 83 a little further to the right), or 245 and 302 to other Underground stations.

To walk back to Wembley Park station, cross over and take Barnhill Road on the left beyond Safeway's car park. Follow Barnhill Road round to the right at a church, left into St David's Close and through bollards on to a tarmac path on the right. This runs through a green strip between railway lines and the flats of the Chalkhill Estate and eventually joins Windsor Crescent. Turn right along Chalkhill Road to Bridge Road and then left to Wembley Park station.

EXTENSION: TO TROBRIDGE HOUSES (1-MILE LOOP)

From the corner of the fence, do not turn right but continue ahead – a waymark on the signpost shows the direction – on a path which bears slightly right to follow the field edge and joins a surfaced track. At another footpath signpost (which points to Valley Drive, indicating a footpath route along the north edge of these fields which brings you near to Kingsbury station), turn right past a school to Slough Lane. Directly opposite are some of the unusual houses designed by Trobridge. Turn left to the group that includes Midcot, just past the pub, and extends round the corner into the main road. E.G. Trobridge (1884–1942) was an eccentric architect in the Arts and Crafts tradition whose houses of the 1920s and 1930s are not just picturesque pastiche but incorporate symbolism in their design, hence the exaggerated emphasis on sheltering roofs or porches. The group on the hill in Bucks Lane seems to echo almost every style and period of English architecture, from Norman castle to Tudor hall.

Cross Kingsbury Road and go up Roe Green opposite or along the edge of the park alongside. At the other end of this small park you may be able to glimpse Roe Green Manor. Adjoining it is a walled garden which is usually open to the public during office hours (Tel. 020 8206 0492 for information on opening hours.) Turn right up Highfield Avenue, noticing the distinctive style of the flats near the top. At the junction with Bucks Lane, pause to look at the astonishing range of architectural features at each corner, such as turrets and mock drawbridges, before turning right down Bucks Lane, taking a quick look at the strange entrance porches down Ash Tree Dell on the right. At the bottom of Bucks Lane, cross to Kingsbury Green and go down Church Lane to the junction with Slough Lane to rejoin the main route.

Pinner and Headstone Manor

Pinner has a short but beautiful High Street, the site of an annual fair which has been held here since 1336. Pinner also has a surprising number of genuine timber-framed farmhouses, in spite of its reputation as typical Metroland, both along the streets and at Headstone Manor. These no longer have any connection with agriculture, but Pinner Park Farm is still a working dairy farm and the view from Wakehams Hill up to Harrow Weald Common is still predominantly rural.

....

DISTANCE: 4.0 miles (circular). Connection with Walk 22 at Brookshill.

EXTENSION: Pinner to Stanmore station via Brookshill (5.0 miles).

TERRAIN: Pavements and rough farm tracks.

REFRESHMENTS: Pubs and cafes in Pinner, tea bar in Headstone Manor barn, pub at Old Redding on the Extension.

TRANSPORT: Metropolitan Line. Buses H11, H12

WALK 21

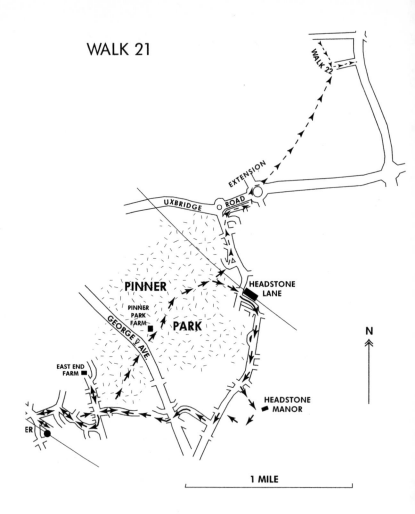

(connects with Piccadilly and Jubilee Lines), H13, 183 (connects with Northern Line).

TRAVELCARD ZONE: 5

STARTING POINT: Pinner station. Pinner High Street for buses.

....

Turn left out of the station, then right and right again up the High Street (WCs down Chapel Lane opposite). This short but colourful street has three fine old pubs, some 18th-century shop frontages, a medieval farmhouse (Church Farm) and a 16th-century building, converted to a wine bar. Turn right at the top in front of the church along Church Lane, which has many cottages of different periods and styles. Just past Pinner House and Ingle Close, turn left up an enclosed path to Moss Lane. Here a short diversion left will bring you to a group of buildings that includes East End Farm and Cottage, the best preserved of Pinner's half-timbered farm buildings, with some features dating from the 15th century. Return and walk up Wakehams Hill nearly opposite the end of the enclosed path. When the road bends right, continue straight ahead on a footpath, through kissing gates and along the left-hand edge of a field up to George V Avenue. Cross this to the main farm drive to Pinner Park Farm, continuing beyond the farm buildings on a fenced earth track which ends at a gate on to a rough surfaced road. *For the route to Brookshill, Old Redding and Stanmore, see the Extension below.*

Turn right along this rough road to Headstone Lane and follow this rightwards for half a mile, then enter the grounds of Headstone Manor on the left. Follow the broad tarmac path ahead past tennis courts, then turn in through a gate to the lovely complex of old buildings: tithe barn, moated 14th-century manor house, granary and small barn. There is much to see here and light refreshments are available in the tithe barn, as well as an exhibition of the area's history.

Returning to the gate, take the tarmac path ahead past the children's playground. When it bends left continue on a gravel path between sports fields and follow it past a small pavilion out to Headstone Lane. Turn left, cross over and take the second turning, Elmscroft Crescent. At the end of this, cross over directly to a small close and continue on the footpath beyond it, past a cemetery, back to Wakehams Hill and Moss Lane. Turn left on Moss Lane and right at Tookes Green past the memorial fountain to see the variety of old and attractive houses which line this end of Church Lane. Continue down Church Lane to the church and retrace your steps to the station.

EXTENSION: PINNER TO STANMORE STATION VIA BROOKSHILL (5.0 MILES)

Through the gate, continue ahead, to the right of a brick-piered driveway, on a hedged grassy path, and up steps to cross over the railway. Pass Chantry Road and take the next turning on the left. Pass the Letchford Arms and continue up Headstone Lane. Cross over and follow the right-hand pavement into Boniface Walk, which follows the Uxbridge Road rightwards to the next roundabout. Your path is on the far side. To reach it, cross the Uxbridge Road, on the pedestrian crossing on the near side of the roundabout, and cross Oxhey Lane by the island towards the fence of a playing field. Follow the fence right for a few yards to take a footpath signposted to Brooks Hill. This climbs up between fields with a lovely view of woodland on the hill ahead. Go through another kissing gate and continue in the same direction up the right-hand side of a large field. The hollows in this field are formed by the springs and head waters of the River Pinn which rises here. Over a stile you approach a farm riding school. Continue between the farm buildings to a white gate. *Here you join Walk 22.* To complete the walk to Stanmore, take the right-hand track down Brookshill Drive and follow instructions from paragraph 8 of the directions in Walk 22. For pub, picnic place and superb view (and perhaps for a brief exploration of Harrow Weald Common and Grimsdyke) take the left-hand track signposted to Old Redding until you reach the pub, with picnic place and viewpoint just beyond to the left.

PINNER FAIR:
Takes place on the Wednesday after the spring bank holiday.

HEADSTONE MANOR (Harrow Museum and Heritage Centre):
Open Wed–Fri 12.30p.m.–5p.m.; weekends and bank holidays 10.30a.m.–5p.m.

Stanmore Circular via Bentley Priory and Harrow Weald

On the fringes of London lie some superb stretches of Green Belt land, preserved as common, park or council-owned open space, sometimes designated as Country Park. This walk crosses several such areas, a remarkable succession of varied landscapes of heath, parkland, woods, farm fields and meadowland grazed by horses and cattle; with cottages, farmhouses, an 18th-century mansion and a couple of extravagant High Victorian houses. The Extension to Canons Park takes you to a more formal 18th-century landscape.

....

DISTANCE: 5.0 miles (circular). Connection with Walk 21 at Brookshill.
EXTENSION: To Canons Park (2.0 miles).
TERRAIN: Hilly. Some paths may be rough and muddy.
REFRESHMENTS: Pubs at Stanmore Little Common, Old Redding and Stanmore (on return).
TRANSPORT: Jubilee Line. Buses 142, H12.

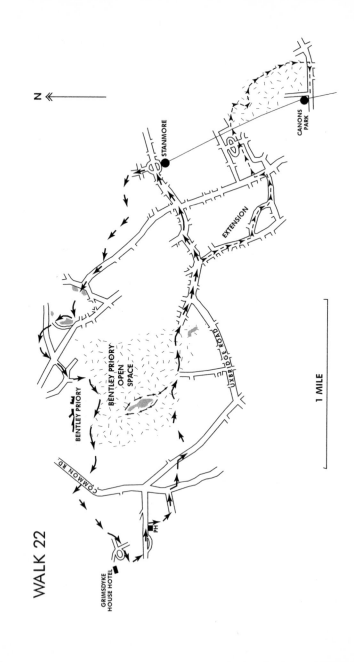

WALK 22

N

GRIMSDYKE
HOUSE HOTEL

COMMON RD.

BENTLEY PRIORY

BENTLEY PRIORY
OPEN
SPACE

UXBRIDGE ROAD

PH

STANMORE

EXTENSION

CANONS
PARK

1 MILE

TRAVELCARD ZONE: 5

STARTING POINT: Stanmore station.

....

From the station, cross the road and go up Kerry Avenue opposite. At the end of the houses, go through a kissing gate into Stanmore Country Park. After a few yards on a broad track, turn left past a brick hut (an electricity sub-station) and follow this path as it winds through woodland, ignoring a crossing path. Just over a small rise, fork left on a path crossing at an acute angle and continue on this, past another path junction to drop downhill through trees. At the bottom of the hill the path meets a crossing path, with a rough plank bridge on the right over a tiny stream. Cross this and climb up this path, north then north-west, ignoring turnings, still in woodland, until the path leaves the trees to cross an open expanse of grass with an imposing mansion visible on the hill above. The path continues briefly through another strip of woodland to a kissing gate leading on to Dennis Lane. Turn right up the road to a junction at Little Common.

Cross the road to a gap in the fence and follow the path round the pond on your left. Facing the gabled cottages, bear right, passing to the right of a black hut and, opposite another row of cottages, bear right to barriers at the end of the track.

For pub and village, turn left in front of these cottages, then right down an alleyway to The Vine pub fronting the main road. On the way you will catch glimpses of the Gothic castellations and turrets of the Victorian Stanmore Hall. Return round by road and pond for a closer view.

Go through the barriers to a sports field and turn left along a footpath beside the rugby pitches. Past the first pitch turn right through birch trees on a narrow path beneath the pitches and beside the Fish Pond. The path follows the bank of the pond, passes to the left of another, then to the right of a cricket pitch and out to Warren Lane. Warren Lane has no pavement, so cross over to a path opposite into woodland. Fork left, cross a tarmac drive and continue to a small car park (WCs here) and back to Warren Lane. Turn right, cross the main road and go down Priory Drive opposite (a right of way in spite of numerous off-putting notices). Follow it round to the right for 75 yards then through gates on the left on to a hedged track and through more gates into Bentley Priory Open Space.

Behind the high security fence lies Bentley Priory. The present house was built in 1775. It was the last house of the Dowager Queen Adelaide and the stream in the valley below was dammed to form a lake beside which a summerhouse was built for her. There is an enclosed deer park on the east side, but cattle graze the open slopes. The whole area is a local nature reserve, managed to preserve its mosaic of woodland, scrub, grassland and damp areas. It is open to the public, though the Summerhouse Lake Inner Nature Reserve is only accessible by a stile at the southern end. The house was Dowding's Fighter Command HQ during the Battle of Britain. It is still owned by the Ministry of Defence and is not open to the public.

Ahead is a map board and signpost. Turn right on the path signposted to Harrow Weald Common. The path is surfaced for wheelchairs, so is easy to follow for 0.7 mile across the Open Space, below the Priory fence and with fine views south. It eventually leaves the grassland through a kissing gate to continue through a rhododendron shrubbery and out through a five-bar gate to a road (bus 258). Cross straight over to a path beside a map board of Harrow Weald Common and drop down on the path. Go ahead past a seat, cross over a plank bridge and turn right immediately before the next plank bridge. Continue down this path for about 70 yards, passing one waymark post until you reach another at a crossing track. Turn left on this track which runs through the wooded common before coming out along the edge with views over open fields on the right.

After passing a group of cottages it bends left to a drive at a gate leading to two gabled cottages. Leave the waymarked path here, cross over the drive and go down the path through the trees for 70 yards. At a plank bridge and No Cycling notice on the left, turn right on a narrow path between holly bushes which soon passes under a magnificent redwood. Just beyond is the drive to Grimsdyke House, now a hotel. It is a fine, elaborate, Tudor-style house by Norman Shaw. Its most famous occupant was W.S. Gilbert, who it is thought to have died while trying to save a young lady from drowning in the lake. Sections of the Dyke itself – a Saxon earthwork from the 5th century – can still be seen in the grounds, across the golf course nearby and, intermittently, beyond to Pinner Green.

Cross the drive, pass another tall redwood and continue on the path through rhododendrons. Emerging from the shrubbery with a bank on the left, climb the bank and another bank beyond to join a waymarked path. Turn left and follow this path round to the Old Redding Road, opposite a car park with picnic tables at a fine viewpoint over to Harrow-on-the-Hill and beyond. Cross over and turn left to the Case is Altered pub. (There are two other pubs with this strange name in this part of Middlesex. It is usually associated with soldiers returning from the Peninsular War and is thought to be a corruption of a Spanish phrase.)

Just beyond the pub, take the wide surfaced track and follow it down to Copse Farm (Suzanne's Riding Stables), where you should bear left before the farmhouse to a tall Public Bridleway signpost. *This is the point of connection with Walk 21.* Follow the Brookshill arm left up a pebbled track, turn right on the road at Brookshill for 100 yards, then left at a lamppost and Circular Walk signpost and follow this path to Clamp Hill. Turn right along this road for 150 yards, then left down Lower Priory Farm drive at another signpost. From the farm gate, take the earthen path on the right alongside a tiny stream along the lower edge of Bentley Priory Open Space. Keep to this path for about half a mile. Where the path passes the top of a street, a footbridge leads back into the Open Space. There is a map board ahead. If you want to visit the Summerhouse Lake, turn left before the board to the farm fence, right to a gate, left over a stile and right over another stile into the Inner Nature Reserve. You can do a complete circuit of this tranquil area. Otherwise continue on the path beside the stream to a footbridge a little further on. Cross the footbridge and walk forward to an open field. The grassy path continues below a line of trees to join a surfaced track at a signpost. Take the path signposted to Stanmore Church, pass the Boot Pond and exit through a gate into Old Lodge Way, which leads to Uxbridge Road where you should turn left. Bus H12 will take you back to Stanmore station, or bus 340 to Canons Park (Jubilee Line) or Edgware (Northern Line) stations.

To walk back to Stanmore station (0.6 mile) cross the road and pass the churchyard, where there are ruins of a 17th-century church alongside St John the Evangelist Church, built in 1849. Beyond Old Church Lane, there is a pleasant public garden with benches and there are two pubs opposite the garden. Continue for 0.5 mile along Church Road, The Broadway and London Road back to the station.

From Old Lodge Way turn left along Uxbridge Road and cross to the two churches, as above, but then turn right down Old Church Lane. After passing several interesting buildings and a college, turn left into The Ridgeway and left again at the end and go down Lansdowne Road. Cross Marsh Lane, turn left then right through high brick gateposts into the original western avenue of Canons Park. Cross the next road and continue over the railway bridge into Canons Park.

In the park, leave the tarmac path as it turns right and go ahead, bearing right at a metal fence, for a view of the Georgian house (which replaced the grander mansion of the Duke of Chandos). The house is now the North London Collegiate School, but much of the original landscaping is still recognisable in the public park. On joining a tarmac path, turn right to the little Temple, then cross the grass to the gate in the high, 18th-century red brick walls. The square walled garden within, originally the kitchen garden, is now the George V Memorial Gardens, with formal beds and a lake in the centre. On coming out of the gardens, turn left to the corner and follow the walls round another two sides. When you reach a crossing track cross the grass ahead to the Spinney. Turn right on the path in the Spinney (this was the south avenue to the house) or follow the parallel line of trees in the open. All the paths come out on Whitchurch Lane at the far end. At Whitchurch Lane, turn left to look at St Lawrence's Church, with a magnificent baroque interior and the 1735 Chandos Mausoleum, or turn right to Canons Park Jubilee Line station. All bus routes go to Edgware Northern Line station.

ST LAWRENCE'S CHURCH, LITTLE STANMORE:
Open Sun 2p.m.–5p.m. during summer;
2p.m.–4p.m. during winter.

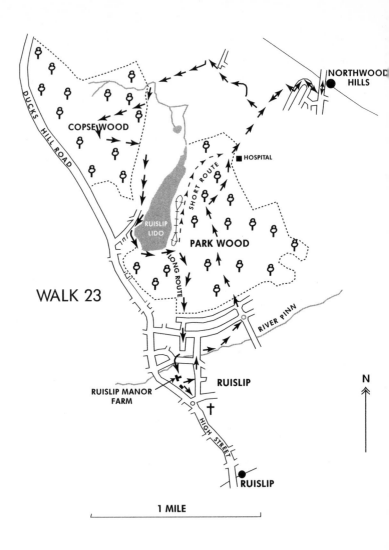

COPSE WOOD

DUCKS HILL ROAD

RUISLIP
LIDO

■ HOSPITAL

SHORT ROUTE

PARK WOOD

LONG ROUTE

WALK 23

RIVER PINN

NORTHWOOD
HILLS

RUISLIP

RUISLIP MANOR
FARM

RUISLIP

HIGH STREET

N

1 MILE

Ruislip Woods and Northwood Hills

To the north of Ruislip lie the Ruislip Woods. This string of woods stretches across 726 acres and can provide a whole day's walking. This walk traverses two of the woods and includes views from the Northwood Hills. The longer route takes in the fine buildings of Ruislip Manor Farm and village.

....

DISTANCE: 4.5 miles (circular). 6.5 miles (circular) via Ruislip.
TERRAIN: Hilly, rough paths, often very muddy.
REFRESHMENTS: Pubs at Northwood Hills and Ruislip village. Restaurant/bar and sometimes refreshment hut at Ruislip Lido. Teashop at Ruislip Manor Farm.
TRANSPORT: Metropolitan Line. Buses 282, H13 (H11 nearby).
TRAVELCARD ZONE: 6. Zone 4 for buses.
STARTING POINT: Northwood Hills station.

....

Cross over the road, turn left, pass the pub then turn right down a footpath out to a street. Turn briefly right, then left down Highland Road, follow it round then go through a gate on the right into a recreation ground. Turn left along the edge by a line of trees, go over a ditch and half right across the second field. At the far end by a corner of a fence, take the right-hand one of three paths. Continue, slightly downhill along the edge of a golf course beside a cemetery. Just before a concrete workshop, turn left on a clear path round a golf green, turn right at a signpost to the 7th tee and immediately right again along a footpath into trees. Cross a stream and go up to the clubhouse and car park, then ahead to a crossing path at metal barriers. Turn left here, with a hedge on your right, and, further along for a short distance, a high fence on the left. Reaching the end of the golf course at a footpath junction, continue and cross a stream on a concrete bridge. Pass a pond then turn left through a kissing gate to cross a footbridge. Continue into a fine, open stretch called Poors Field and walk down between two stretches of woodland.

Just past a bench, ignore a bridleway waymark and take the footpath a few yards ahead on the right. Go through the gate and up the path into Copse Wood ahead. Continue to climb steadily through woodland for 0.5 mile, ignoring a turning, until you meet a stony crossing track. Turn left here, still uphill, to the next path junction. (Here, a right turn would take you beyond Ducks Hill Road to Mad Bess Wood and beyond that to Bayhurst Wood and right out into the open fields above the Colne Valley – a splendid route into the countryside.) Instead, turn left downhill through the woods for 0.3 mile, joining other paths but continuing in the same direction to a gate back out into the open at Poors Field. Turn right on a path that climbs a little then drops down, with the Ruislip Lido coming into view. Ruislip Lido was built in 1811 to top up the Grand Junction Canal and was later put to recreational use. Pass an information board and turn left to go round the restaurant to the side facing the water (bus H13 from the road beyond).

Continue round the edge of the reservoir. At the far end there are benches and a shelter overlooking the sandy beach, with WCs and a refreshment hut, the Railway Room (open seasonally).

Opposite is the Ruislip Lido Railway. (You can take a ride on the railway to Haste Hill. Go out through a gate on to a broad fenced track, turn right and rejoin the route at the point where the long and short routes join up.)

Go out beside the turnstile into Park Wood.

For the short route, turn left and follow the path beside the Lido Railway fence for about 0.5 mile until, some 100 yards after a path joins the track at an acute angle, another path turns off as you are approaching the end of the woodland with a golf course ahead. Turn uphill on this path, climbing steadily and forking left to reach the top of the hill near hospital buildings.

For the longer route via Ruislip, take the path ahead to the left of the information board. At a junction of paths, continue ahead and cross a broad bridleway. (A line of pylons used to stretch right across the wood at this point.) Continue in the same general southerly direction, ignoring a left fork and a crossing path. When you reach some houses, continue on a path alongside them, with the houses on your right, and out to a road opposite Sherwood Avenue. Go down Sherwood Avenue and at the end, take a path on the right through a small coppice out to a road at a bridge. Cross over, cross the grass to a roadway and take a path on the left leading to Ruislip Manor Farm. The buildings include the 16th-century Manor Farm, the Little Barn of the same period, now a public library, the magnificent Great Barn, probably dating from the 14th century, and the Norman motte and bailey site. The cow byre, rebuilt after a fire, houses a tearoom and art exhibitions. A panel on the library wall gives some details of the buildings, which were still in use as farm buildings until the 1930s. Before continuing, walk down past the bowling green and duck pond, and out past the WCs to look at the village buildings clustered near the church at this end of the High Street. (Ruislip Metropolitan/Piccadilly station is 0.5 mile down the High Street.) Go past the timber-framed building overlooking the churchyard (built in 1570 and later adapted to make two rows of five back-to-back dwellings), past the church out into the High Street. Turn right up Bury Street as far as the 17th-century Mill

House, returning by the path between the Great and Little Barns to continue the walk. Go through the gate of Manor Farm House, pass to the right of the house, turn left on the road, cross a bridge over the River Pinn and turn right through a gate into a wide strip of grass bordering the river. Follow the Pinn through two fields to Kings College Road – you will need to cross the second one half left as the gate is to the left of the brick pavilion. (The path beside the Pinn the other side of the road continues to Eastcote.) Turn left up the road and go back into Park Wood. Go straight ahead up the main track for 0.7 mile. Side paths help avoid the worst of the mud in wet weather. At the top, as the path ahead drops downhill, turn right along a bridle path and fork left to reach the top of the hill near hospital buildings.

The short route continues here. Continue, with a high wooden fence on your right, out to the open hillside with long views over woodland and hillside. Keep along on the top of the hill alongside a hedge. The path drops gently to return to the corner of the fence, with a line of trees on the right, where you rejoin the outward route. Go half right down the field out to the road to return to the station.

RUISLIP LIDO RAILWAY:
Open Sun all year.
Weekends, Tues, Wed, Thurs April–Oct.
Daily June–Aug and during school holidays.

WALK 24

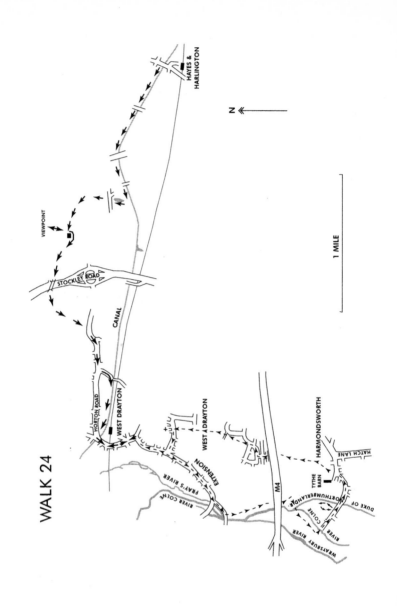

HAYES & HARLINGTON

VIEWPOINT

STOCKLEY ROAD

CANAL

HORTON ROAD

WEST DRAYTON

WEST DRAYTON

FRAY'S RIVER

EXTENSION

RIVER COLNE

M4

HARMONDSWORTH

HATCH LANE

TYTHE BARN

DUKE OF NORTHUMBERLAND'S

RIVER COLNE

WRAYSBURY RIVER

N

1 MILE

Stockley Park by canal to West Drayton and Harmondsworth Moor

Stockley Park is an example of the creation of a new landscape out of degraded land – usually after gravel extraction followed by infilling with refuse – by a partnership of local authority and business. At Stockley Park, a golf club and a business park have paid for the transformation of 250 acres of derelict rubbish tip into a country park, with paths winding between golf greens and wild flower meadows, young woodland and viewpoint hillocks. Harmondsworth Moor, on the Extension, is another example of these new landscapes, like Bedfont Lakes near East Bedfont.

....

DISTANCE: 3.7 miles (linear). Connection with Walk 25 at West Drayton.

EXTENSION: To Harmondsworth Moor (2.5 or 4.0 miles).

TERRAIN: Gravel paths.

REFRESHMENTS: Pubs in Hayes, bar and cafeteria in Stockley Park, pubs and cafes in West Drayton. Pubs in

Harmondsworth on Extension.

TRANSPORT: Thames Trains. Buses 90, 140, 195, E6, H98, U1 (Mon–Sat), U4.

TRAVELCARD ZONE: 5 and 6. Zone 4 for buses.

STARTING POINT: Hayes and Harlington station.

....

From the station turn right down station Road to the bridge over the canal. Cross the bridge, turn right down steps to the towpath and turn right under the bridge. Continue along the towpath for a mile, passing under three more bridges (steps beside the second one – a new brick bridge – lead up to The Woolpack pub). Beyond the third bridge, the high fence of Stockley Park begins. At a seat and canal information panel, turn through a kissing gate into the park on a broad gravel path beside a reed-fringed stream. This leads to a sheet of water fed by two weirs, overlooked by some of the business park buildings. Cross a road to the gravel path to the right of the 11th tee and, when this divides a few yards on, continue on the middle path, signed Pedestrian Footpath, climbing gently through a wild flower meadow and young woodland, bearing left when this path meets another. It continues through the golf course, dropping to cross a hollow on boards and heading towards the golf clubhouse ahead with its striking curved roof.

At a path junction, ignore the path going directly to the clubhouse – this is for golfers only. This walk continues round to the left, but it is worth climbing first to the viewpoint on the man-made grassy hillock a short way up the main path on the right. On a clear day, the view ranges from Canary Wharf to Windsor Castle. Return, pass the clubhouse, and turn right up to a roadway for a few yards, then up a gravel track between the far side of the clubhouse and the car park. To visit the building, go up the steps and through a glass door ahead on the right, then upstairs to the public bar, cafeteria and WCs. There are panels on the walls which give details of how the derelict refuse tip was transformed (with the help of 1.6 million worms!).

Continue on the gravel path beyond the car park as it winds its way through young plantations to the dramatic suspension bridge – its single arch support visible from much of the park – which carries pedestrian and bridle paths over the Yiewsley Bypass. On the far side, follow the main track ahead, just beneath a viewpoint. Beyond the hillock, fork left on a path parallel with a horse track. Ignore a right fork just past the children's adventure playground. At a crossing track at the far end of the park, go out through a gate on the right on to Horton Road.

It should be possible to reach the canal through the section of park opposite. If the park is fenced off, as at the time of writing, turn right and walk through the industrial estate to Horton Bridge Road. Turn down past the Brickmakers Arms (a reminder that brick earth was dug out of this area before rubbish was tipped in) towards the lovely old canal bridge, and down steps on the right to the towpath. Turn right for 0.3 mile to the next bridge. *Connection with Walk 25 from this point.* Go up to the road, turn left to cross the bridge and continue up the High Street to West Drayton station, just before the railway arch.

EXTENSION: TO HARMONDSWORTH MOOR (2.5 OR 4.0 MILES)

Continue under the railway arch down station Road past shops, then turn right down Swan Road to The Swan pub. (The church and 16th-century gateway of the demolished Manor House are a few minutes' walk down Church Road on the left. You pass them on the return route to West Drayton.) Continue along the edge of The Green, which is lined by a variety of attractive old houses, and carry on down Mill Road. Where the road bends right over an elegant bridge, with Old Mill House beyond and the mill wheel visible beneath the adjoining buildings, turn left down Cricketfield Road, past the Anglers Retreat pub. Walk along Fray's River and continue for about 100 yards. Just before the road crosses the River Colne on a metal bridge, turn through a kissing gate on the left into the Harmondsworth Moor Country Park. Continue on a narrow path through bushes. This soon opens out and continues as a grassy path through a wild area beside a pond. This leads to newer, gravel paths across a more open area. Fork right and continue over a footbridge and under the M4. Keep to the right of a large lake, where lapwings and coots nest, and turn right away from the lake on a path signposted to The Ring. Cross a wooden footbridge over the Colne and fork left on a path beside it, continuing on another path until you reach a broad, rough crossing track, opposite the entrance to a further section of the country park (not yet open at the time of writing). Turn sharp left, crossing the river again on a narrow pedestrian bridge. Continue ahead as the track becomes a road (Moor Lane), going between bollards to keep in the same direction for several hundred yards to the next wooden gate leading to the park on the left. This is the only entrance to this section of the park.

For an optional loop, go through the wooden gate, take the right-hand facing path and keep along the edge by the willow-fringed river. This is the Duke of Northumberland's River, one of the many channels of the Colne, natural and man-made, which contribute to this watery landscape. Across the river you soon have an impressive view of the length of the Harmondsworth Tithe Barn (191ft) and the church tower beside it. Beyond the little amphitheatre lined with stones from the old Waterloo Bridge (the amphitheatre is used by the park rangers for educational work), the grassy path beside the river ends at a rushy pool. The gravel path curves round, passing several stiles which give access to a fenced plantation. (Climb the first stile, turn up steps and so on round to more steps to reach the centre circle with seats in an area designed to attract butterflies.) The main path continues past a small pond and picnic tables, over a low footbridge and back to the entrance gate.

Almost opposite this gate is one leading into Waterside, with the offices of British Airports Authority who have provided this park. This 40-acre section is also open to the public and it contains the Rangers Office and Visitors Centre. To visit this, go through the gate and bear right at the lake opposite the offices. Continue down the right-hand side of the lake, past an exit into Accommodation Lane to a small staff car park. The visitor centre will be in or near the low grey buildings beyond.

Back on Moor Lane, cross the bridge and continue down the road to the tiny, triangular village green of Harmondsworth, overlooked by the Five Bells pub and the even older Sun House. The jewel of the village is the tithe barn, thought to have been built in the 1420s. You can see it across the courtyard through the gates of Manor House Farm behind the Five Bells, or from the churchyard. It can be visited only by prior arrangement. The church has a carved, early Norman doorway and an 18th-century cupola on top of a part-medieval, part-Tudor tower. Before leaving the village, turn down Summerhouse Lane opposite the Sun House to have a look at a couple of grand houses, the Hall and Harvard House, previously the Grange.

To finish the walk here, continue down the High Street to the corner with Hatch Lane. Turn left for the U3 bus back to West Drayton, or cross over for a bus to Heathrow Central/Piccadilly Line station.

To return to West Drayton, go through the churchyard and bear right to an exit between stone pillars at the far corner. Follow the path from here across fields, passing the other end of the lake, to a footbridge over the M4. Continue in roughly the same direction through a small housing estate, bearing right up Rowan Road and following the footpath on the left of the green. Go past houses and a school and then across a field (The Closes) to reach Church Road opposite the church, the cupola of which makes a useful landmark. Turn left to Swan Road and retrace your steps to West Drayton station or buses.

HARMONDSWORTH MOOR COUNTRY PARK:

At the time of writing, only some sections of the 288 acres are open. The remainder will open during the course of 2000. There will be a leaflet guide available from the Hillingdon public libraries and from the visitor centre. For further information, ring the Rangers Office (020 8738 8571).

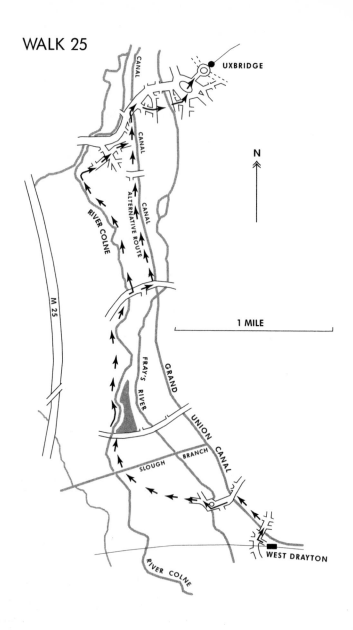

WALK 25

N

UXBRIDGE

1 MILE

CANAL

CANAL

CANAL

ALTERNATIVE ROUTE

RIVER COLNE

M 25

FRAY'S RIVER

GRAND

UNION CANAL

BRANCH

SLOUGH

WEST DRAYTON

RIVER COLNE

West Drayton to Uxbridge via Little Britain

An excursion through another part of the Colne Valley. If you are lucky, you may see horses fording the wide shallows of the river at Little Britain. The walk crosses into Buckinghamshire to go alongside Huntsmoor Park before returning to Middlesex and continuing on the riverside path or the canal towpath.

....

DISTANCE: 4.0 miles (linear). Connection with Walk 24 near start, Walk 17 at end.

TERRAIN: Mostly gravel paths, with some earthen stretches.

REFRESHMENTS: Pubs and cafes in West Drayton and Uxbridge. Tea hut at Little Britain Lake.

TRANSPORT: Thames Trains. Buses 222, U1, U3.

TRAVELCARD ZONE: 6. Zone 4 for buses.

STARTING POINT: West Drayton station.

....

From the main entrance turn left down the station approach road to the High Street. Turn right and continue as far as the canal. Cross the bridge over the canal and immediately turn right down to the towpath. *Walk 24 joins here.* Turn right under the bridge and walk along the towpath to the next bridge. Go up steps here, turn left over the canal and along Trout Road, crossing over Fray's River. Follow the road round to the right, then after a few yards turn left through a gate with a bridleway signpost next to it (sometimes hidden in trees). Continue along this enclosed path, which has pleasant views over open water to your left.

After 0.5 mile, the path rises to cross the Slough Arm of the Grand Union Canal. It drops down again through a wild area and runs along the River Colne until it reaches Little Britain Lake at a wide, shallow ford. Packet Boat Lane, which crosses the ford, takes its name from the pub The Paddington Packet Boat on Cowley High Road, half a mile up the road on the right, which used to be a port of call for canal boatmen. (The tea hut is a couple of minutes' walk up the road, opposite Old Mill Lane.) There are fishermen's paths all round the lake.

Walk between the lake and river to the footbridge just ahead. Cross the footbridge, then turn immediately right on a gravel path with the farm fields of Huntsmoor Park on your left and the Colne on your right. The path crosses a stream on a wooden footbridge and continues mostly through woodland. Shortly after crossing a tiny stream on a concrete bridge, it meets another path coming from the open park (a right of way from Ford Lane). Turn right and continue through woodland again to a bridge. Go up the steps to Iver Lane. Turn right over the bridge back into Middlesex.

There are two routes from here into Uxbridge. (The path along the River Colne has the more rural views, though it runs alongside factories. It is a narrow, earthen path with sections that could be tricky in wet weather. It can also be rather nettly in summer.)

For the alternative route along the canal towpath, continue down Iver Lane (do notice the ironwork gate with farm implement motifs at the corner of Old Mill Lane) to the canal bridge, and turn left on the towpath for nearly a mile, passing underneath Cowley Mill Road.

For the River Colne route, turn left immediately after crossing the river bridge down a path beside a factory, sign-posted Public Footpath, and follow the rough path beside or near the river for 0.8 mile until a stream joins it. Here the path is forced to turn right and follow the stream to a rough road. Continue in this direction, pass a pub, cross a road and go down Culvert Lane, past some terraces of cottages, to turn left on the canal towpath. *The canal route rejoins here.*

Pass the General Eliott pub, go under the road bridge and turn up on to the bridge. Cross the bridge and turn right opposite the Dolphin pub down Waterloo Road and left into Frays Waye. Cross the small recreation ground, go over Fray's River and up to Cowley Road. Turn left, cross at the traffic lights to a road opposite, to the left of a small green space. Cross over Cross Street to Windsor Street, which leads to Uxbridge High Street and the Metropolitan and Piccadilly Line station, with the bus station behind.

Carry On Walking

There are many green routes through London devised by local authorities or other bodies. Here are the details of the guide leaflets for routes mentioned in this book.

....

CHESSINGTON COUNTRYSIDE WALK:
For a free leaflet, send an s.a.e. to:
Lower Mole Countryside Management Project, Highway House, 21 Chessington Road, West Ewell, Surrey, KT17 1TT.

HILLINGDON TRAIL:
A leaflet pack is available from any branch of Hillingdon Public Libraries (£2) or by post (£2.50). Tel: 01895 250 200.

HOGSMILL WALK:
For a free leaflet, send an s.a.e. to:
Kingston Environmental Services (Parks Dept), Guildhall 2, Kingston upon Thames, Surrey, KT1 1EU.

WEST LONDON WATERWAY WALKS:

A pack of six walk leaflets (£2) is available from: Ealing Parks and Countryside Services, Perceval House, 14–16 Uxbridge Road, Ealing, London, W5 2HL.

THE LONDON WALKING FORUM:

This is a partnership of over 80 amenity organisations and local council departments. Its aim is to establish green routes that are adequately waymarked and have a clear, descriptive route leaflet. The Forum is developing two circular walks: the Capital Ring through Inner London and the LOOP (London Outer Orbital Path) on the outer fringes, but within reach of London's public transport system. The LOOP is well advanced. There are leaflets available for all eight of the sections south of the Thames, and for several north of the Thames. For further information on what is available and sources for other self-guided walks leaflets, ring the London Walking Forum (020 7213 9714) or visit their web site www.londonwalking.com.

RAMBLERS ASSOCIATION:

If you would like to join others in a country-type ramble within Greater London with a volunteer leader, ring the Ramblers Hotline (020 7370 6180) for the programme of Saturday strolls. The walks are between five and seven miles and take place on alternate Saturday afternoons anywhere within the London Travelcard area. They are free of charge and are organised by the Ramblers Association Inner London Area for the general public.

Ask at your local library or ring the Ramblers Association national office (020 7339 8500) for the address of your nearest RA Local Group. Some have local as well as country rambes on their programmes.